SPIRIT OF ASIA

Michael Macintyre

INTRODUCTION BY

David Attenborough

BRITISH BROADCASTING CORPORATION

Published by the
British Broadcasting Corporation
35 Marylebone High Street
London W1M 4AA

ISBN 0 563 17791 8

First published 1980

Endpaper map drawn by David Worth

Printed in England by
Balding and Mansell
Wisbech, Cambs

Colour separations by
Scan Kolor, Ilkley, England

PREVIOUS PAGE Folk dance of the
hill-tribe people, north of Chiang Mai, Thailand

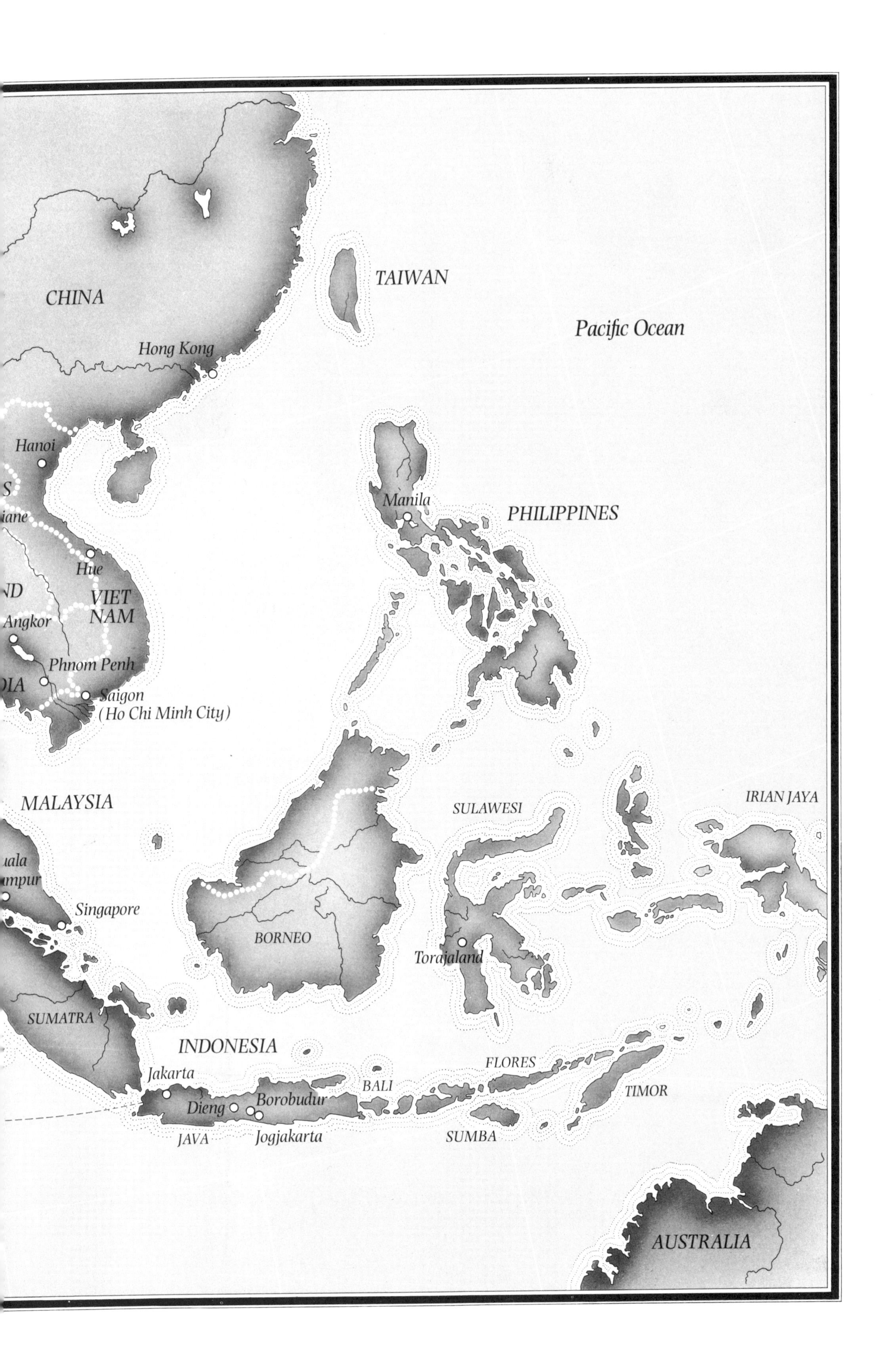
CHINA
TAIWAN
Pacific Ocean
Hong Kong
Hanoi
Hue
VIET NAM
Angkor
Phnom Penh
Saigon (Ho Chi Minh City)
Manila
PHILIPPINES
MALAYSIA
Singapore
BORNEO
SULAWESI
IRIAN JAYA
Torajaland
SUMATRA
INDONESIA
Jakarta
Dieng
Borobudur
Jogjakarta
JAVA
BALI
FLORES
SUMBA
TIMOR
AUSTRALIA

SPIRIT OF
ASIA

For Clive,

Thank you for the nice things you said — but then, you always were my favourite narrator!

With love,

Michael

CONTENTS

INTRODUCTION
David Attenborough

Three great rivers, the Irrawaddy, the Salween and the Mekong, flow down from the south-eastern corner of the Tibetan plateau. They surge southwards between India to the west and China to the east, threading their way through mountains covered by rhododendron forest, cutting their gorges deeper and deeper. Eventually, they emerge on the flatter, lower lands and there they slow and begin to meander. Sometimes they almost cease to move at all. The Mekong becomes so swollen during the height of the rains each year, and flows so slowly, that one of its tributaries can make no forward progress whatever, reverses its current and flows backwards to spill over the land through which it has just travelled, forming an immense seasonal lake. As the rivers wander across the plains, they drop the sand and mud that they had first picked up a thousand miles to the north, when they were travelling at speed, and extend their deltas still further into the shallow waters of the South China Sea and the Indian Ocean.

The land does not come to an end here totally but in the west is prolonged as a single hooked finger, the Malay Peninsula, which curves southwards to touch the equator and then, broken only by a few narrow straits of sea, extends beyond in a long chain of volcanic islands that reach out eastwards for a further thousand miles. The sea around these fragments of land is so shallow that only a small drop in the level of the world's oceans, such as might be brought about by locking up water in larger polar ice-caps, would expose dry land between them and the continent. Indeed, in recent geological times this happened. It was then that the islands acquired most of their animals. Rhinoceroses reached Borneo, Sumatra and Java. Tigers managed to get as far east as Bali. Beyond that point, however, the Asian connection ends. A naturalist leaving Bali and entering Lombok quickly notices the change. There he sees for the first time white yellow-crested cockatoos, and in Sulawesi, farther east still, a strange slow-moving monkey-like creature, the cus-cus, which carries its young in a pouch like a kangaroo. He has at last left Asia behind and entered the faunal world of Australia.

This land, with its pendant chains of islands, has been given many names by Europeans. Once they called it the East Indies, that is to say, the land beyond India. Later, the mainland part of it became Indo-China, a reasonable label bearing in mind its neighbours, but one which seems to deny its inhabitants their own identity. Currently, the collective name most used is scarcely more than a dry compass direction – South-east Asia. The names of its constituent parts have also altered as the people escaped from alien domination of one kind or another and claimed their own independence. Siam now prefers to be known as Thailand, Cambodia as Kampuchea, and Tonkin and Annam, between them, form North and South Vietnam. In the island chains that are now for the most part the republic of Indonesia, several islands have been renamed: Borneo has become Kalimantan, and Celebes is called Sulawesi.

When it was that men first came to South-east Asia we do not yet know. The sodden soils of tropical jungles are poor preservers of bones. Most decay and crumble to nothing within a few years. But a few exceptional remains have been found to prove that human beings were here at a very early date indeed. A skull cap and leg bone found in Java in 1891 belonged to a man who lived there over half a million years ago. He was not anatomically identical with ourselves but a somewhat ape-like precursor. Our own species, which we have so immodestly called Homo sapiens, 'wise man', was certainly here about 40,000 years ago. Bones and stone tools of such a date come from several places including the vast cave of Niah in north-west Borneo. The people who lived there were roughly contemporary with the early men in Europe who chipped flint and hunted mammoth. But whereas Europe has altered radically since those chill times when glaciers covered most of northern Europe, the land round Niah has remained almost unchanged. Pollen grains trapped in peats and muds demonstrate that the plants that grew then still thrive in the surrounding jungle and the bones from the people's refuse tips are almost all of animals that are still hunted by local people today. The South-east Asian jungle, in fact, is one of the most ancient surviving communities of plants and animals in all the world.

Some 5000 years ago – and some authorities believe it may have been even earlier than that – the South-east Asians acquired the skill of working bronze. They cast knives and hoes, socketed axe-heads and, in particular, superb drum-shaped gongs two feet across. The richest finds of such objects have been made at Dong-son in North Vietnam and this site has given its name to the whole culture, but bronzes dating from this time have been found in many parts of the area. The largest of all the ancient gongs is still preserved in Bali where it has been given its own special shrine, for the people believe that it dropped from the sky and credit it with intense supernatural powers. The designs on such gongs and other pieces strongly suggest that the people who made them believed in a life after death and in a world of spirits. Certainly such animistic beliefs still survive in those parts of South-east Asia away from the mainstream of travel and trade – among the Batak in the mountains of central Sumatra, in Sulawesi among the Toraja, and in the remote parts of Bali itself. Even in those countries, such as Burma, where later more sophisticated faiths have long been officially adopted, the ancient belief in spirits still lies only just below the surface of people's thoughts.

Then, some 2000 years ago, the great cultures of India and China began to grow in power and to spread their influence into the land between them. The Chinese sent armies to conquer Tonkin and Annam, and in the soils of Dong-son the local bronzes are abruptly replaced with pottery and metal objects that are unambiguously Chinese. The influence of the Indians was apparently a more peaceful one. They called the land to the east of them, revealingly, Suvarnabhumi, 'the Land of Gold', and it was the lure of treasure that made them set up tiny trading stations all around the coast of the mainland and along the sea routes through the islands. India had by this time brought together the vast number of animistic beliefs that flourished among its peoples and united them into the single comprehensive body of philosophic thought that we now call Hinduism (the name means no more than 'from the Indus'). It is the oldest of the world's great faiths. It spread rapidly and pervaded every aspect of the people's lives so that, even today, the music and dancing, the literature and the folk tales of much of South-east Asia can only be properly understood by reference to their Indian origins. By the sixth century AD, temples to Hindu gods were being built in Burma and Java.

About the same time, Buddhism too came to these lands. The faith, which had also originated in India, had reached China during the first or second centuries AD, travelling across Central Asia along the Great Silk Road. Chinese traders now brought it to South-east Asia. But the Indians themselves also carried it across the Indian Ocean from the land of Buddha's birth. Small bronze Buddhas have been unearthed in Sulawesi, Thailand and Malaya; and in Java stands Borobudur which today is one of the most important of all surviving Buddhist monuments. A third and final religious contribution came from India only 500 years ago. Indian traders brought Islam to Java, Sumatra and Malaya, where it conflicted with Hinduism just as it did in the Indian subcontinent itself, and eventually, in most of Indonesia, supplanted it.

Europe belatedly became aware of South-east Asia when Marco Polo returned from China at the end of the thirteenth century and told of campaigns waged by the Chinese against barbarian kingdoms to the south of their frontiers. Thereafter Europeans came to regard this distant region as a gigantic and mysterious treasure house, just as the Indians had done centuries earlier. In the early seventeenth century, Mercator's Atlas described it, wonderingly, in the same stately prose that was being used at the time for translating the Bible.

> 'There is great store of gold and silver in the country and precious stones and pearls which the sea casteth up upon the shore. For it hath an abundance of beryls, adamants, carbuncles and pearls. Here is silk enough to furnish all the world. There are great store of elephants. And great dragons in the wilderness that are as big as elephants and do fight continually with them. And dogs as fierce as lions. And great store of serpents which the inhabitants do roast and eat and a kind of ants which they eat with pepper as we do crayfish. Here are white apes and chamaeleons which were heretofore thought to live by air.'

Since those times, European countries – Britain, France and Holland – have pursued their quest for such wealth to the extent of dividing up the region between them and annexing separate territories into their empires. Today those empires have all fallen and the countries, nominally at least, have regained their independence. To the European traveller the land remains as beautiful and mysterious as any in the world. Other continents and cultures have been shorn of their glamour by the aeroplane, but not these magical lands. I first went to them to look for the animals that live in the forests – the azure-winged fairy blue bird, argus pheasants, orang utans and gibbons – and the strange, unique creatures that have evolved in the isolated islands of the Indonesian chain – the barbirusa, a grotesque wild pig on Sulawesi, a pure white starling in Bali, and the largest living lizard , the so-called dragon of Komodo, a tiny island east of Sumbawa. But though animals first drew me there, it was the people and the landscape that they have created that have drawn me back again and again.

There is something particularly poignant about a countryside in which men have, by sustained and intensive labour over many centuries, managed to reach a truce with nature, where they have not smashed the natural world but instead have succeeded in working with it to build something so harmonious that it seems eternal but which is, in reality, dependent upon a subtle partnership. You can sense such a feeling on the downlands of southern England, which were created by ancient shepherds and the grazing habits of their sheep, and in the vineyards of Mediterranean Europe, but nowhere is it more moving than on the hillsides of Bali or Sulawesi, where terraces have been built, tier upon tier, each meticulously laid out so that water floods them to just the right depth and is channelled from one to the other, trickling through bamboo conduits and cascading in a thousand tiny waterfalls. In these fields, for thousands of years, men have been planting out the emerald green rice seedlings, tending them in the baking sun as they suck up the water and grow with a speed that is almost visible.

The partnership, however, is not always a permanent one. Sometimes man, for various reasons, withdraws and leaves nature to resume its own course. In the fifteenth century AD the Khmer people of Cambodia abandoned Angkor, one of the most stupendous temple complexes ever built by man. The jungle swiftly reclaimed it. Even today, some parts have been allowed to remain within its grip. The intertwining roots of fig trees clasp gigantic stone faces, trunks heave up the paving of the long, deserted corridors and shoulder aside the columns. Borobudur in Java was also once similarly buckled and riven. Archaeologists discovered that its interior, over the past thousand years, had been washed away so that the whole monument was in danger of collapse. So now its lost earthen heart is being replaced by ferro-concrete. Eventually it will regain its original shape but it will have lost something of its essence and no longer will its tilting terraces and moss-covered friezes make visible the passage of time.

Over the past quarter of a century, the world's most dreadful catastrophes have ravaged the beautiful, haunted lands of South-east Asia. Foreign powers have urged on the armies of the people and sent their own to assist them in rushing to destruction. No country in either World War suffered such intensive bombing, such wholesale slaughter. Even far away from the war zones, the West has made itself felt. And yet, in spite of it all, the ancient traditions have remained strong. Although orientalised versions of western popular music are heard everywhere, echoing from transistor radios in the smallest village and through the courtyards of temples, the musical traditions still flourish. The instruments the people use include drums, bamboo flutes and fiddles, but most are made of bronze. Some are gongs which have an ancestry reaching back to the great bronze gongs of the Dong-son. Big ones are hung singly, smaller ones placed in racks. Bronze keys are laid in rows in instruments like metallic xylophones. All these instruments play together as a gamelan. With as many as forty players, it is, apart from the western symphony orchestra, the largest consort of musical instruments used by man. The sound it makes has been likened to moonlight pouring over fields. 'The gamelan gilds the time,' a Dutchman wrote. 'The hours forget their usual course. The quarters shrink to golden minutes, minutes seem like blissful hours.' To these ravishing sounds, puppeteers in the markets or the temples still recount the legends of the Hindu epics as images of Hindu heroes, cut out of leather, cast their flickering shadows on a screen; and dancers who once performed for kings and princesses still continue to create visions of ethereal beauty. The piety that erected the vast golden pagoda in Rangoon, and the talents that designed the stately terraces of Borobudur and shaped the exquisite heavenly goddesses on the walls of Angkor, mercifully still flourish to delight all who wish to see.

TRIBAL LANDS OF INDONESIA

'The World of Shadows'

Indonesia consists of a vast archipelago of 13,677 islands strung out in an equatorial chain between the Indian Ocean and the Western Pacific, a distance of 4000 miles. It is a land of powerful contrasts and astonishing beauty. From island to island, dense tropical rain-forest alternates with low swampland and open savannahs. Above emerald-green rice fields, lofty volcanoes pour smoke into the sky. On high plateaus sulphurous hot-springs bubble noisily beside cascades of icy water.

The people of Indonesia – some 139 million – are as richly varied as the landscape; with 366 distinct ethnic groups speaking at least 250 different dialects the country is an ethnologist's paradise. Every one of the world's major religions has taken root here, and yet the old beliefs remain, together with a way of life which has changed little in 5000 years.

The land which is Indonesia was inhabited by early man as much as 400,000 years ago. The sea-level was then much lower than today, and a natural land-bridge connected Java and Sumatra with the continent of Asia. It was probably by way of this bridge that prehistoric man, 'Pithecanthropus', reached Indonesia. At the end of the Glacial period the sea-level rose, forming the present-day island groups, but the migration of peoples continued, spreading through the islands by means of rafts and primitive canoes. Today the hunting and gathering cultures of that age, the Mesolithic, still survive in Indonesia among tribal groups hidden within the jungle and mountainous interiors of the larger islands – the Punans of Borneo, the Toalas of Sulawesi, and the Kubus of Sumatra – and they still practise the shamanistic spirit worship of those far-off times.

Later waves of migration, beginning around 2000 BC, brought the ancestors of the present-day Malay peoples of Indonesia, driven from the mainland areas of Burma, Cambodia and Vietnam by pressures from the north. With the first wave came the neolithic proto-Malays, who brought a primitive knowledge of agriculture to the interior regions and mingled with the non-Malay population already established. With the second came the deutero-Malays, a more advanced people who settled in coastal areas. From this amalgam of races, a distinctive pattern of life began to emerge, with the cultivation of rice, pottery-making, and skill in working bronze and iron, as elements common to tribal groups scattered far and wide across the archipelago. They also shared a religious belief in the spirits of nature and the ghosts of

The village of Praigolli, north-west Sumba island

ancestors, whom they honoured by erecting megalithic monuments – great columns and slabs of stone. Today their descendants, the 'Ancient Peoples', maintain those early beliefs, and the stones which stand imposingly in front of their houses are still treated with the greatest respect.

Sumba is a small barren island situated half-way between Bali and Timor, celebrated for its sturdy breed of horses and the beauty of its traditional 'ikat' weaving. In small villages built on hillsides high above the rice-fields, tall houses cluster around groups of stones, resting places for the spirits of the departed. Remarkably, in a nation dominated by Islam and with its fair share of Christian missionaries, two out of every three Sumbanese persist in worshipping the spirits.

Each year on the seventh and eighth days after the full moon of February and March, and just before dawn, the shores of Sumba are invaded by a horde of multi-coloured sea-worms, appearing as if by magic. To the people of Sumba it is divine revelation, and from the behaviour of the worms they believe they can foretell the future. If the worms nip when gathered, this portends a scourge of vermin which will devour the crop; if they break when touched, this augurs that the crops will rot from an overabundance of rain; but if the worms are their normal slithery selves, the year's harvest will be plentiful.

The extraordinary phenomenon of the sea-worms, the 'nyale', is explained by a well-known creation myth of Sumba. Long ago, during the reign of Raja Wulan, King of the Moon, the people were decimated by drought and famine. Anxious for the well-being of his subjects, the king appealed to the high priest to determine the cause of this national calamity and to implore the gods to have mercy on his people. Divination revealed that a human sacrifice was necessary. Raja Wulan had one daughter, a beautiful young maiden, with flowing hair reaching to the ground, and it was decided that she, Ratu Nyale, should be the sacrificial victim, that she should be ritually dismembered and the parts of her body cast into the sea as offering to the gods.

The sacrifice was duly performed and the gods were appeased, and in reply they magically transformed the body members into food so that the famine should cease. From the tibia they made shark, from the rib-cage turtle; the liver became squid, the fingers octopus, and the feet crabs; lobsters came from the toes and eels from the intestines. And the gods made sea-worms of many colours – blue worms from her hair, red worms from her blood, yellow worms from her sirih-stained lips. And from that time to this, the 'nyale' worms return once a year to remind the people of the heroic martyrdom of Ratu Nyale.

The gathering of sea-worms and the reading of portents are the responsibilities of the 'ratu-ratu', the priests or shamans, invested on these special days with such spiritual power that none may cross their path. As they make their way to the sea they are accompanied by dog-spirits of the 'Merapu', the ghosts of god-like ancestors, who will bite anyone who enters their sacred space, inflicting mortal illness or insanity. Villagers take care to keep out of their way.

For the Sumbanese, the arrival of nyale marks the start of a new year and it is immediately followed by 'Pasola', a ritual fighting on horseback using blunted spears. The Pasola has its origins in the need to shed blood to ensure the fertility of the earth in the year ahead, and even today, despite the blunted tips, many riders are injured in the battle, and there is rarely a year when no one is killed. When this happens it is considered as divine punishment for offending the ancestors.

New Year is the occasion for purification, for the expiation of sins and the exorcism of demons, when inhibitions and frustrations may be given an outlet through accepted forms of ritual aggression. The Pasola is one such outlet, and the 'Pajura', ritualised boxing, is another. This takes place beside the sea, as the moon rises the night before the sea-worms are due to arrive. Before the fight begins the right hand of each combatant is wrapped in blades of wild grass with a cutting edge capable of producing vicious wounds, and again serious injuries are not uncommon.

These violent rituals are a reminder that less than a hundred years ago the Sumbanese were head-hunters. There are still old men in the villages who remember how severed heads were boiled, the skin and brains removed, and the skulls displayed on the 'Adung', a symbol of the cosmic tree of life. Since the head contains 'life-force', capturing heads from a rival clan served to increase the overall life-force of one's own. This practice continued well into this century, in Sumba as in other remote parts of the Indonesian archipelago ruled by animism and ancestor-worship.

The small, mountainous island of Nias lies on the equator, just off the west coast of North Sumatra. It is separated from Sumba by some 1600 miles, but in religious belief and the expression of that belief in art, the two cultures are strikingly similar, particularly in their use of large stones as monuments and sacrificial altars. Linked with the idea of an after-life, these megaliths are the tie between the living and the dead, and they provide a focus for the religious life of the village. In Nias they stand directly in front of the chief's house: finely tapered obelisks, massive stone slabs, and enormous tables and chairs, seats for spirits of the dead, everything carved with the greatest precision and delicacy. Megalithic art flourished in Nias as nowhere else in Southern Asia, and, even more remarkably, persisted, together with head-hunting, into the present century. Even today the erection of a new stone is accompanied by a great ceremony, with the sacrifice of pigs and the famous Nias war dances, everything designed to increase the prestige of the chief and obtain for him a higher rank in the hereafter.

According to the old beliefs, the chiefs of Nias were the reincarnation of the forefathers who came down from heaven, and they enjoyed a god-like status among the people of their own village. Important matters relating to social and religious custom were openly debated among the commoners, but it was always the chief who had the last word, and his decision was binding. It was he who adjudicated in matters of law, and who chose a punishment to fit the crime. Today it is the law of Indonesia which applies, but only forty years ago an offender would have been judged according to tribal law, the severest punishment being reserved for crimes against the forefathers. Offences against women fell into this category because the ancestor-spirits were interested above all in the continuity of their own family lines, and pre-nuptual virginity was therefore of the greatest importance. A man may have lost his hand for the offence of touching a woman's breast, and both man and woman would probably have lost their lives if she had become pregnant.

The chiefs continue to wield considerable power among their own people, and they still live in magnificent wooden houses built by slaves in the middle of the last century. The houses rest on massive wooden piles, two feet in diameter, and they have high roofs which soar above those of other houses in the village to proclaim their exalted status. It took several years to build such a house, and human sacrifices were required to mark every important stage in the construction. Inside, the walls are decorated with fine wood-carving, and there are long rows of wooden pegs for the jaws of pigs slaughtered at the ceremonial feasts. The chief may also possess a row of small wooden statues of the ancestors, made in the belief that spirits of the deceased continue to maintain contact with the living and influence their destinies. After death, a wooden image of the dead man is carved, and his spirit transferred into it in the form of a spider. On such occasions as a birth or a death, the image is offered the sacrifice of the lungs, liver or heart of a pig, to ensure the good will of the spirit it contains. The carving of these ancestor figures is Nias art at its finest.

In neighbouring Sumatra, among the Batak people of Lake Toba, animism also went hand-in-hand with a megalithic culture and great skill in carving wood. Their most outstanding works of art are the 'magic wands', long wooden staffs delicately carved with human and animal figures, and variously used for divination, rain-making, and to induce illness and death. According to legend, the magic wand was the outcome of the incestuous love of a twin brother and sister. Forced to flee their village they became imprisoned in a tree of the forest, together with a variety of animals and the priests and teachers sent to find them. The tree was brought back to the village, where it stood before the house of the rajah, the living souls still confined within their petrified wooden forms. From this magical tree smaller copies were made, each wand possessing a similar magic of its own.

After a wand had been carved, a special ceremony of dedication was required. For this, a small boy was kidnapped from a hostile village and given hearty meals and palm wine, so that his soul would be favourably disposed towards his captors. After some weeks of such hospitality he was buried in the ground up to his neck and again given food. But instead of wine, molten lead was poured into his mouth from a buffalo horn. While still warm, his brain was taken from his head and used to prepare a magical substance 'pupuk', which was then placed inside the topmost figure of the wand. Without pupuk a wand would have been as impotent as a gun without bullets, but with the magic paste in position it was transformed into a weapon of great power.

Like the people of Nias, the Toba Batak surrounded their villages with high stone walls, and filled them with benches, tables and chairs, all carved from stone for the convenience of the ancestors. When a high-ranking Batak died he was buried for a year and then exhumed, the skull and bones being placed in an immense sarcophagus together with those of many previous generations. The sarcophagi were boat-shaped, with a monstrous protective face carved like a figurehead on the prow. Today they appear to float on the grass, an anchored fleet of solid stone.

A similar effect is found in Sulawesi, in the land of the Toraja, but here it is the houses of the people, not their sarcophagi, which appear to be floating. The Toraja explain that this is no accident. When their ancestors came to Sulawesi from the west they came by boat. Deciding to stay, they pulled their vessels ashore and converted them into houses. Whatever the reason, Toraja houses certainly resemble ships in appearance, and they are an impressive sight as they stand in long rows facing their rice granaries.

Toraja houses have high-soaring front porches, and a central pillar usually adorned with buffalo horns, trophies of their elaborate funeral ceremonies and the most important bestower of status on the family living inside. The funeral ceremony of a high-ranking family is likely to last three weeks and include the sacrifice of 200 buffalo. A complete village must be erected around the ceremonial field to accommodate the guests – perhaps 10,000 or more – who will participate in the processions and provide an audience for buffalo-fighting and dancing. When all is finished they will return home with their appropriate share of sacrificed buffalo meat, and the temporary village will be burned to the ground.

The Toraja bury their dead in cliff graves, and nearby they place a life-sized effigy of the deceased, usually in a gallery of wood or rock alongside the effigies from earlier funerals. Sometimes an effigy is given a travelling bag for his journey to the Land of Souls, a land where everyone continues to live as he did on earth, accompanied by the souls of buffalo sacrificed at his funeral. To the Torajans the wholesale destruction of worldly wealth which is a feature of these gigantic funerals is more apparent than real. Transferred to the hereafter, it will ensure the dead of an influential position there.

Throughout Indonesia, the worship of spirits is so firmly rooted that it influences the lives of everyone, be they Muslim, Christian, Buddhist, or, as in Bali, ostensibly Hindu. The religions of India and the West would have had little impact on South-east Asia had they been unable to incorporate in some way the animistic beliefs of the native people, and this is nowhere better shown than in Bali, where offerings are given daily to gods and spirits alike. Thirteen hundred years ago, when Indian religions were just beginning to gain acceptance in Bali, the native 'Bali Aga' people were being terrorised by a giant king called Sang Mayadenawa, who prevented them from performing their religious ceremonies. In desperation they sought help from the Aryans of India, and in the fierce battle which ensued Sang Mayadenawa was killed. But many of the Aryans also died in the fighting, and today they are remembered as great heroes and their spirits revered as gods. In the New Year festival of Kuningan, the Balinese re-enact the battle against Sang Mayadenawa, the oppressive tyrant, in the 'Fight of the Gods'. Small images representing the spirits of the dead heroes are placed in boxes, and each one is carried on a palanquin borne by eight men. During the afternoon, a procession of the palanquins winds its way from the temple down to the river, for a ceremony conducted by the priest. When they return to the temple, the bearers are in trance, and the crowd scatters in alarm as they begin to charge violently around the temple courtyard, possessed by the spirit of the god they are carrying. To bring the ceremony to a close, the palanquin bearers are forced back inside the temple, no easy matter since a man in trance is possessed by the strength of five ordinary men. But once inside, a sprinkling of holy water from the priest is enough to bring them back to normal.

As in Sumba, this ritualised battle is essentially an outlet for pent-up aggression. The demons are cast out, the soul is purified, and another year begins.

Sunrise in Praigolli village, Sumba. The goats are standing on large stone slabs, which are seats for spirits of the dead

High priests of Sumba, the 'ratu-ratu', harvesting the sacred sea-worms, 'nyale', at the New Year festival of Pasola. Early in the morning on two days of the year, and precisely synchronised with a particular phase of the moon, the worms converge on the shores of Sumba as if by magic. From the condition of the worms as they are caught the ratu-ratu make predictions about the coming year

When the ratu-ratu return from harvesting the worms, the villagers keep well clear of them. On holy days such as this, the priests are invested with great spiritual power and are accompanied by dog-spirits of the Merapu, the ancestor-gods, which will inflict a mortal wound on anyone who comes near

OVERLEAF The ritual battle of Pasola

Immediately following the harvest of nyale worms, a hundred horsemen converge on the beach and begin the ritual battle of Pasola. Divided into two teams, they charge one by one towards the opposing side and, when they have come within a range of ten to twenty metres, they hurl their wooden spears with great violence. The spears have blunted tips but they are thrown with such force that they can easily break a man's skull. It is not uncommon for a horseman to be killed in the Pasola.

The Pasola battle from horseback is essentially a fertility rite. Like the cock-fight, it is designed to shed blood on the earth, a sacrifice to the gods to ensure the fertility of the soil during the coming year

On the night preceding the Pasola, the strongest men of the village gather on the beach and bind their right hands with sheaves of wild grass. At the rising of the moon they form into opposing teams, and the Pajura begins. A form of ritualised boxing in which the sharp blades of grass will cut into an opponent's face and so cause blood to fall on the sand, the Pajura is, like the Pasola, a fertility rite. When the fight is over, the men pair off with village girls who have been watching them and vanish into the night. At this one time of the year they are permitted a degree of sexual licence which at any other time would be forbidden.

During the celebrations of Pasola a young dancer wears around her neck a gold pendant with an ancient design representing the female reproductive organs – vagina, ovaries and womb

Fishermen on the south coast of Nias, a small island in the Indian ocean close to north-west Sumatra. Nias is separated from Sumba by some 1600 miles of the Indonesian archipelago, but the two islands have in common their religion – a belief in the spirits of nature and ancestors – and their use of megaliths – slabs and obelisks of stone, memorials to the dead and, at the same time, ceremonial seats and altars for the ancestor-spirits

ABOVE A family house in the north of Nias

OPPOSITE The chief's house in Hilinawalo village, south Nias

The population of Nias is concentrated in two areas at opposite ends of the island. There are few roads, and it requires a long boat trip to travel from one end to the other. Consequently the two regions are relatively isolated from each other and are strikingly different in appearance. In the north the houses are built on an oval-shaped ground plan and scattered throughout the village. In the south they stand imposingly in long rows on either side of a broad avenue paved in stone. They have a rectangular ground plan, square fronts and high, soaring roofs. The house of the chief of Hilinawalo is particularly imposing. Built early last century, it rests on gigantic piles, each of which required a human sacrifice after being placed in position

ABOVE Houses at the centre of Hilinawalo village. Their appearance is said to resemble the shape of the Portuguese galleons which came to Nias for trade in the 16th century. At the front of each house is a large living-room with a raised platform. From here the people can gaze out at the street through a long wooden grill stretching the width of the house

OPPOSITE Stone slabs, giant tables and obelisks, memorial stones and seats for spirits of the dead, stand in front of the chief's house in Bawomataluo village, south Nias

Hilinawalo. Young girls use bamboo tubes to carry water from a spring to their hill-top village

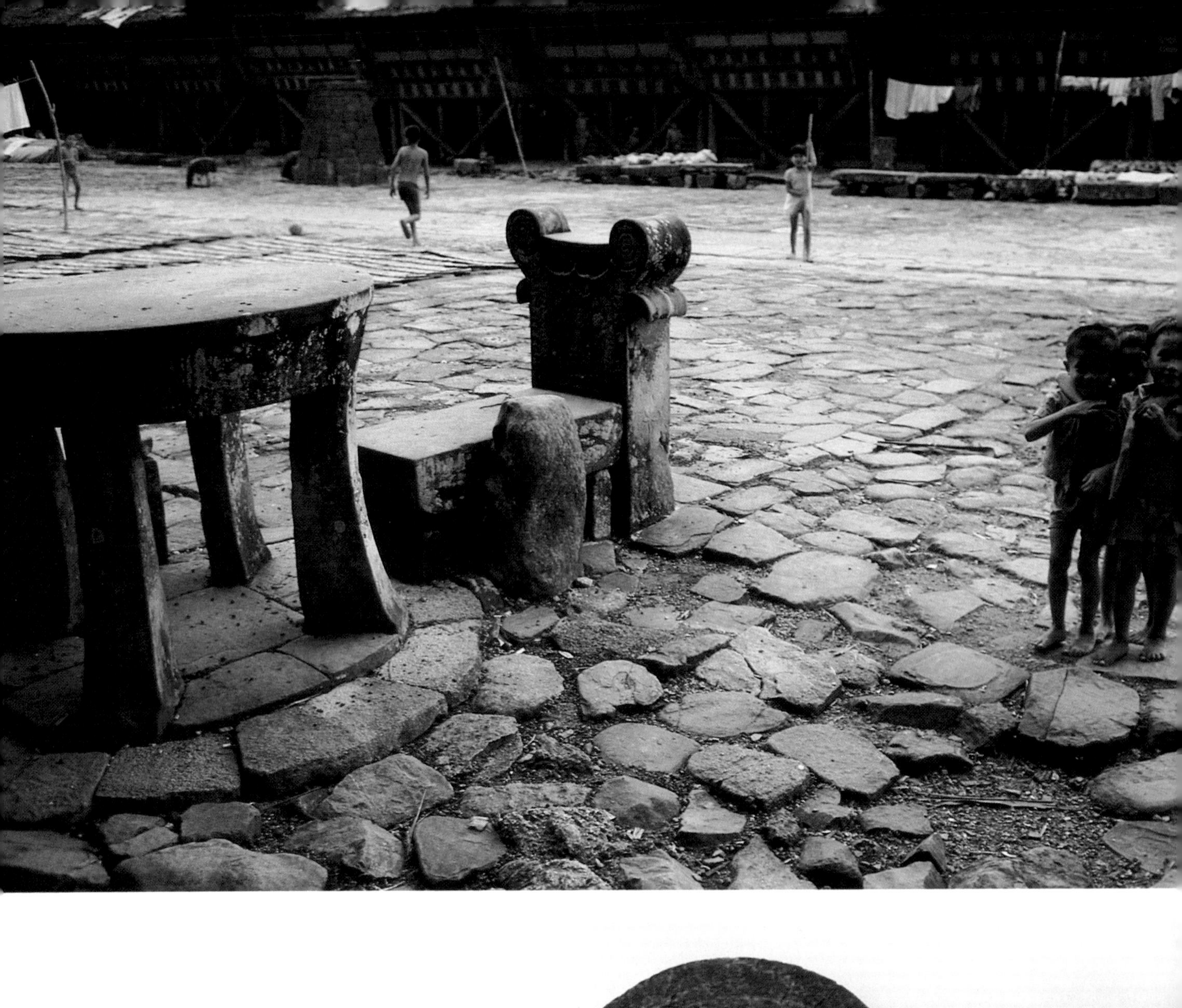

ABOVE Decoration on a large stone slab in front of the chief's house in Bawomataluo village. In south Nias, the art of the megalithic age developed to a state of perfection unequalled anywhere in the world and, remarkably, was still producing fine carvings at the start of this century

OPPOSITE A giant table and chairs for the use of the ancestor-spirits, and the entrance stone to the village, Hilisimaetano, south Nias

The wood carvers of Nias possessed a skill to rival that of the stone-masons. These fine statues, about 56 cm in height, represent ancestors, and they were made in the belief that spirits of the deceased continue to maintain contact with the living and influence their destinies

The villages of Nias today present a mixture of cultural influences, and of the old and the new, which is bewildering. Well into the 20th century, the men of Nias were courageous warriors who frequently embarked on warlike missions against neighbouring villages to capture slaves or the heads of their enemies. The megaliths are the most solid reminder of those days, but the old men of the villages still recall head-hunting missions, and enact the rituals which surrounded them, though instead of human heads they now use a crude likeness fashioned from coconuts

The stone jump, a feature of the larger villages of south Nias, was originally a device for training warriors: a successful head-hunting expedition demanded the ability to vault over the walls which fortified Nias villages. But the stone jump also served to eliminate the feeble: behind the jump, wedged between the paving stones, were upturned points of spears ready to impale a would-be warrior who could not quite make the distance

The Batak, distantly related to the people of Nias, are similarly skilled in wood-carving. These small figures, approximately 5 cm high, adorn the stoppers of containers for the magical substance 'pupuk'. Prepared from the brain of a child-slave killed by being forced to drink molten lead, the pupuk was used to imbue ritual implements with magic potency

Masks were used to impersonate ancestor spirits in funerary rites. This one represents Singa who accompanies the spirit of the deceased to the world of the dead

OPPOSITE Batak skill in carving stone is best displayed on their sarcophagi, which are boat-shaped and contain numerous skulls and bones of dead rulers

In common with the people of Sumba and Nias, the Toraja of Sulawesi are by tradition believers in the spirits of nature and their ancestors. Here, too, large stones are an integral part of religious worship, and sometimes act as tethering posts for buffalo during a ritual sacrifice.

Toraja houses have towering front porches (opposite) with a central post displaying an array of buffalo horns, trophies of funeral ceremonies during which a great many buffalo are sacrificed. Facing the houses are the rice stores (left), finely decorated with abstract patterns and buffalo motifs. For the Toraja, buffalo are the chief bestower of status both on earth and later in heaven. When a Torajan dies, the spirits of buffalo sacrificed at his funeral go with him to paradise

The Toraja bury their dead in cliff graves. Beside them, alongside earlier effigies standing in galleries cut from the rock face, they place an effigy of the deceased. Drab and poignant, they are like an audience at a theatre for the dead

The funeral effigy of a prince of Langda village. Unlike traditional effigies, this one is extremely lifelike since the sculptor, who had studied naturalistic carving in Bali, worked from a photograph to capture a true likeness.

The widow must stay beside the coffin throughout the first week of the funeral festivities, accompanied from time to time by her grandchildren

The funeral ceremony of a high-ranking man is likely to last three weeks, and a complete village must be erected around the ceremonial field to accommodate the guests, perhaps 10,000 or more, who will take part in the processions and provide an audience for buffalo-fighting and dancing

ANIMIST BALI

Beneath the ostensibly Hindu religion of Bali there is a powerful undercurrent of animism and ancestor-worship. Once a year, in the 'Kuningan' festival, this is strikingly demonstrated by the 'God-Fight' of Paxabali village. Small images representing the spirits of dead heroes are placed in boxes, and each one is carried on a palanquin borne by eight men. The bearers are in trance, possessed by the spirit of the god they carry, and they charge violently around the temple courtyard, careering into one another and causing the crowd to scatter in alarm

BALI
'The Morning of the World'

Bali is a small volcanic island of extraordinary natural beauty lying due south of Borneo and a little to the east of Java. Whilst neighbouring islands are now almost completely converted to Islam, Bali is unique in having preserved its ancient Hindu-Indonesian heritage to this day, with a richness of cultural life unequalled anywhere in the world. In Bali, it seems, nearly everyone has creative talent, whether as painter, sculptor, dancer or musician, and yet the Balinese have no word for 'art' as such.

The traditional art of Bali is created as an offering to the gods, who are ever-present and must be treated with respect at all times. In Bali every day is a holy day. Thus religious worship, and therefore art too, are matters of daily concern and an inseparable part of daily life.

The focus of religious and artistic activity is the temple festival, and hundreds take place every year. On any day, a tour of the island is likely to discover at least half a dozen of these colourful events in full swing: long processions of women in their finest sarongs, with huge piles of beautifully sculpted rice-offerings balanced on their heads, an arena crammed with men excitedly placing their bets on the cock-fight about to begin, and, in the distance, the shimmering sound of a gamelan orchestra with its sonorous gongs and tinkling xylophones.

The Balinese have a special talent for theatrical expression in the form of dance-dramas, often with singing and dialogue added, and these too are best enjoyed at a temple festival. Usually they take place at night, the time when magical forces are at their most potent and when the spirits may be summoned to take part in the drama by entering the body of an actor in trance.

In 'Sanghyang Dedari', the Dance of the Holy Angels, two small girls are lulled into trance by the smoke of incense and the slow incantations of a priest. Behind them a chorus of women chants the Sanghyang song, asking the spirits of celestial nymphs to descend from heaven and dance for the people. The little girls are lifted on to men's shoulders, and there they begin to dance in perfect unison, even though it is dark and their eyes are closed. Magically, they are able to execute movements of a dance they have never been taught. When the chanting ceases, the girls simultaneously drop to the ground in a swoon.

The Sanghyang dance is not intended as entertainment – it is a religious dance of exorcism designed to

Off the coast of Sanur, south Bali

rid the community of evil spirits, and the little girls who perform it are treated with the special respect reserved for those who converse with the gods. They are always very young, for a virgin child is considered holy, and the younger she is the closer is her soul to heaven.

For the same reason, the dancers chosen for Bali's most feminine and graceful dance, the 'Legong', are girls aged between five and eleven, but unlike Sanghyang Dedari, this is not a trance-dance, and the tiny dancers must undergo a physically arduous course of training before they are ready to perform in public. Traditionally, the home of the Legong is the 'puri', the palace of a village nobleman, and this serene classic dance has been nurtured within the royal households for centuries. It tells the story of the thirteenth-century King of Lasem who abducts the maiden Rangkesari and locks her into a house of stone. Rangkesari's brother, the Prince of Daha, learns of her captivity and demands her release. The king refuses and sets out to give battle, but on the way he meets a bird of ill omen who predicts his death, and in the fight which follows he is killed.

The story is vigorously enacted by three small girls, tightly bound from head to foot in gold brocade and wearing crowns of frangipani blossoms. At first, they stand rooted to the spot as if in trance, then suddenly they dart forward and begin to circle the courtyard, weaving this way and that, an arm stretched out ahead of them, their eyes staring into space as if in amazement at a phantom only they can see. Their movements are rapid and exact, every flash of the eyes, each snap of the neck being precisely synchronised with the complex rhythms of the gamelan orchestra. The audience, densely clustered around the temple courtyard, is likely to include whole families, old women and young children watching with equal fascination the movements of a dance they know by heart. In Bali, where dancing is concerned, everyone is a connoisseur.

The Balinese world is one of sharing and belonging, and nearly every activity is given group expression, whether it be in family ceremonies, temple festivals, cock-fighting, making music, bathing, bringing in the harvest, or simply the day-to-day affairs of the village. A young child soon discovers that he belongs not only to his immediate family, but to a certain clan, caste, community, and to the Balinese people as a whole, and in each category there is a code of behaviour to which he must conform. He must know the correct clothes to wear for ceremonial occasions; in bathing he must choose a part of the river not too close to that used by the women and he must avoid looking in their direction. When he comes of age he must consent to the painful ceremony of teeth filing, a custom originating in ancient rites of initiation. Caste rules are still of great importance in Bali, though less rigid than those of India. In meeting a nobleman, a commoner must switch from everyday Balinese to a higher form of the language, and at all costs he must avoid making love to a woman of higher caste, a crime punished in the past by being tied in a weighted sack and thrown into the sea.

Ever conscious of their social standing, the people of Bali also have a strong sense of racial identity. A Balinese who marries a foreigner is no longer truly Balinese. This intense feeling of belonging, together with the all-pervading influence of a religion which nobody seriously questions, have led the Balinese to regard their small island as the world itself. Their awareness of other nations seems to affect this feeling not in the least – they are simply irrelevant. In mythology, they picture their island resting on a turtle which floats on the ocean, the tranquil centre of an ordered universe:

'From chaos, through meditation, the world serpent Antaboga created the turtle Bedawang, the stabiliser, on whom he coiled two serpents as the foundation of the world. On the world there rests a lid, the Black Stone. There is no sun, nor moon, nor light in the cave below the stone; this is the underworld whose god is Kala.

'Kala created the light and earth on which flows

a layer of water. Above this are skies, high and low. One of mud, which dried to make the fields and mountains. Then the floating sky – the clouds enthroning Semara, god of love. Beyond lies the dark blue sky with the sun and moon, palace of the Sungod Surya. Then the perfumed sky, beautiful and full of rare flowers where live the awan snakes, the falling stars. Still higher, a flaming heaven of ancestors; and above all the skies live the divine guardians who keep watch over the heavenly nymphs.'

In another account of its creation, Bali was once a flat, barren island. When Java converted to Islam, the Hindu gods moved to Bali in disgust. Since there were no dwelling places high enough for their exalted status, they created mountains, one for each of the cardinal points – Batur to the north, Batukau to the west, Bukit Petjatu in the south, and, in the place of honour, the highest of all, Gunung Agung, in the east. Today Gunung Agung is regarded as the Navel of the World, the Cosmic Mountain, Mahameru.

The Balinese believe the natural world to be held in balance by the opposing forces of good and evil, and this eternal conflict is acted out in their dramatic performances by two remarkable characters – Barong and Rangda. Barong – 'Lord of the Forest' – is the protector of mankind, a fantastic creature with the face of a tiger, four legs, and a high, waving tail. Rangda is his formidable adversary, the queen of witches, controller of the powers of darkness. The masks of Barong and Rangda are themselves 'sakti', magically powerful, and they are kept in special enclosures within the temple, surrounded by offerings. The Rangda mask is considered so dangerous that it is covered by a white cloth to contain its magic.

When Barong and Rangda meet at the climax of a play, it is never sure which of them will emerge triumphant. The actors wearing the masks are in trance, possessed by the spirits of the two adversaries, and everyone present is in a state of great excitement, since the well-being of the village is at stake. If Rangda is victorious, her black magic will be a threat to the whole community. To avert this disaster, men armed with krisses rush to the defence of Barong, but the witch casts a spell which makes them turn their daggers back on themselves. In reply, Barong makes the men invulnerable to their own stabs, and it is one of the most extraordinary sights of Bali as the men, in a powerful trance, vainly attempt to plunge the daggers into their own bodies. Though the outcome is uncertain, the most likely result is stalemate; Barong and Rangda survive to continue the struggle another day.

The Balinese have good cause to respect the forces of nature. They live on the slopes of active volcanoes. Earthquakes are frequent, and sometimes strong enough to destroy a village completely. And they are ever-mindful of July 1963 when the highest volcano, Gunung Agung, erupted, killing 2000 people and leaving 150,000 homeless.

At the time of the eruption, preparations were being made for 'Eka Dasa Rudra', the biggest and most important of temple festivals, which is supposed to take place every hundred years at Besakih, the Mother Temple of Bali. Besakih is dramatically situated half-way up 9000-foot Mount Agung, dwelling place of Shiva, God of Destruction. When smoke started to pour from the mouth of the volcano and the ground began to shake, the people knew they had aroused the wrath of the mighty god, and were now to suffer for it unless he could somehow be appeased. Rather than flee the lava, already sending up clouds of steam as it approached along the river beds, the people knelt down and prayed, and their prayers were answered when, only a few hundred yards ahead of them, the lava flow miraculously came to rest. These people survived but others were not so lucky, and many died from the toxic gases and scorching heat which preceded the lava.

Twenty-four years were to pass before another attempt was made to celebrate Eka Dasa Rudra. On this occasion Shiva was to permit the festival to proceed without interruption, but first it was necessary to rid the island of corpses, by the traditional means of cremation. Until the body is cremated, the spirit of the dead man is unable to leave it and restlessly hovers around nearby. Eka Dasa Rudra could not take place until all such spirits had been set free.

The Balinese cremation ceremony, especially the cremation of a prince, is the most spectacular of its kind to be seen anywhere in the world. Enormous towers of bamboo are constructed and decorated with tinsel and coloured paper. They represent the Balinese conception of the cosmos: a wide base, symbol of the foundations upon which the world rests, then three platforms, the mountains and forests, and above them a plain vertical section, representing the space between heaven and earth. In this section there is a platform to carry the corpse from the house to the cremation ground. The upper portion of the tower consists of a series of receding roofs like a pagoda to represent the heavens. These are always in odd numbers which vary according to the caste of the family: one for Sudras, the common people, from three to eleven for the aristocracy, but none at all for the highest caste, the Brahmanic priests. At the back of the tower is a gigantic head of Bhoma, the Son of the Earth, a wild-eyed, fanged monster with enormous outstretched wings spreading some ten feet to either side. For royal cremations the towers are often so large and so heavy that teams of men, working in relays of 200 at a time, are needed to carry them to the cremation ground. They go in a wild stampede, twisting and turning and careering from one side of the road to the other. In this way they hope to confuse the spirit, and prevent it from finding its way back to haunt the house it had lived in. On arrival at the cremation ground, the body is transferred to a sarcophagus – for a prince this takes the form of an enormous wooden bull with hide of black velvet and lavishly decorated with gold leaf. The bull, and the tower soaring above it, make a magnificent sight, but there is little time to enjoy it. After a final blessing from the priest the pyre is set alight and within minutes the tower is reduced to ashes. The bull, originally hewn from a tree-trunk, takes much longer to burn, and it is so arranged that the burning corpse drops out below the stomach, where it then hangs from wires for all to see.

> 'Strange as it seems [wrote Miguel Covarrubias in his book *Island of Bali*] it is in their cremation ceremonies that the Balinese have their greatest fun. A cremation is an occasion for gaiety and not for mourning, since it represents the accomplishment of their most sacred duty: the ceremonial burning of the corpses of the dead to liberate their souls so that they can thus attain the higher worlds and be free for reincarnation into better beings . . . . A man in Bali is born into a superior state – a higher caste – if his behaviour on this earth has been good; otherwise he will reincarnate into a lower stage of life to begin over again the progressive march towards ultimate perfection. A man who is guilty of serious crimes is punished by being reborn, often for periods of thousands of years, into a tiger, a dog, a snake, a worm, or a poisonous mushroom . . . .
>
> 'At cremation ceremonies hundreds and even thousands of dollars are burned in one afternoon in a mad splurge of extravagance by a people who value the necessities of life in fractions of pennies.
>
> 'The grand send-off of the soul into heaven, in the form of a rich and complete cremation, is the life-ambition of every Balinese. He looks forward to it, often making provision during life with savings or property that can be pawned or sold to finance his cremation . . . . A rich cremation adds greatly to the prestige of a well-to-do family, giving occasion for gay, extravagant festivities that are eagerly anticipated despite the financial burden they represent.'

That was written in 1937, but it is equally true today. The cremation of Tjokorde Agung, the Prince of Ubud village, took place in January 1979, shortly before Eka Dasa Rudra. He was a wealthy patron of the arts, an influential figure in the cultural life of

Bali, highly respected and well loved, and his cremation was of a grandeur appropriate to his status. The overall cost was estimated by his family to be in excess of $60,000.

During the two-month period of Eka Dasa Rudra, every man, woman and child in Bali capable of the journey made the pilgrimage to Besakih temple, bringing with them their offerings and their prayers. Dancers came up from the villages with their percussion orchestras – the gamelan – with forty or fifty musicians, and by day and night performed their sacred dances within the temple enclosure – 'Pendet', a dance of offering, 'Gambuh', an ancient dance-drama, and 'Baris Gede', a slow and stylised war-dance.

As the festivities approached a climax, a huge procession bearing images of the gods made its way from the temple, down between the terraced hillsides, towards the sea fifteen miles away. At the end of the day, sacrifices of bullocks were made simultaneously at chosen sacred places across the island. One bullock was drowned in a lake, another in the ocean, while a third was carried to the summit of Mount Agung and thrown into the crater, an offering to Shiva. This was the prelude to the climax of the ceremonies at Besakih – the great sacrifice of Eka Dasa Rudra. Not only bullocks, chickens and pigs were to be sacrificed, but also birds, snakes, spiders, flies. In fact, the intention was to include one of every species known to the Balinese natural world: there was an alligator in a long wooden box, a baby tiger in a bamboo cage, and an eagle – 'Garuda' – which had apparently volunteered as a sacrificial victim by flying down from the mountain-top and allowing itself to be caught. The sacrifice at an end, the high priests from all parts of the island, twenty-one of them, joined together in a ritual chant of holy liturgies. Their prayers were directed to Sanghyang Widi Wasa, the Balinese Trinity of great gods. Their purpose – to purify the universe.

Near the sacred spring of Tampaksiring a narrow stream tumbles between hillsides densely sculpted with rice terraces. The irrigation system on Bali is ancient but remarkably effective. It relies totally on the gravity feed of water from great lakes in the mountains, down through a network of dams and canals to the rice-fields below

Besakih, the Mother Temple of Bali, perched high on the slopes of a sacred mountain, the volcano Gunung Agung, home of Shiva, God of Destruction

OPPOSITE A High Priest, or 'Pedanda', chanting the holy mantras for a temple festival at Besakih. He accompanies his chanting with an expressive sign language of the hands, the 'mudras'

The great temple festival 'Eka Dasa Rudra' takes place at Besakih only once in 100 years. During a two-month period every man, woman and child capable of the journey comes to the temple with offerings and prayers. At the climax of the festival many animals are sacrificed: one of every species of Bali's natural world. The purpose of the sacrifice is the ritual purification of the whole universe

OVERLEAF The steps of Besakih temple festooned with umbrellas in readiness for the festival of 'Eka Dasa Rudra'

ABOVE One of twelve men dressed in magic black and white cloth for 'Baris Gede', a sacred and greatly stylised war dance only performed at cremations and temple festivals

OPPOSITE The cock-fight is an integral part of a temple festival. Blood spilt on the earth will, it is hoped, please the gods and ensure a good harvest in the coming months. But the cock-fight is a social as much as a religious ritual, and so important a part of village life that it is permitted in Bali whilst being banned in other parts of Indonesia

In Batubulan a sculptor carves an owl from a block of stone, while in nearby Ubud a final coat of paint is given to the giant puppets 'Barong Landung'. In Bali art is so much a part of daily life that nobody thinks it extraordinary if a peasant farmer is also a fine musician or if a girl at work in the fields becomes at night a graceful dancer

Just as the mountains are the dwelling places of the gods, the sea is the home of monsters and demons greatly feared by the people of Bali, who rarely venture far from the shore. But even sea monsters deserve respect, and long processions bearing offerings are a common sight on the south coast of the island

OVERLEAF Sunset over the temple of Tanah Lot

ABOVE A young dancer of 'Baris' dramatises the emotions of a warrior preparing for battle

OPPOSITE During the night Barong continues his journey from village to village, driving before him the demons and evil spirits who lurk in dark places, always ready to cause mischief

OVERLEAF At an all-night temple festival in Batubulan village, 'Djauk', a demon-dance, establishes an atmosphere of heightened excitement as the sacred Barong and two witches prepare to do battle. Each mask is invested with a magical potency which causes the dancer who wears it to enter trance, possessed by the spirit he is to impersonate

Sunrise at Sanur, South Bali

The ancient watering place at Goa Gajah. One of the most important discoveries of Balinese archaeology, it is believed to date from the eleventh century

The Balinese have been skilful in confining tourist traffic to one corner of the island, where roads are well made and the people ready to receive visitors. But isolated among the rice fields are villages which rarely see a tourist, and here the charm of the people is quite unspoiled by the commercialism which governs the coastal resorts

ABOVE Barong emerges from the cave of Goa Gajah where he has spent the night. The cave is very old, probably dating back to the 11th century. Framing the entrance is the gaping mouth of a monster, believed to represent Barong's adversary, the witch Rangda

OPPOSITE The vivid paintings on the ceiling of the Hall of Justice in Klungkung contrast the punishments of hell awaiting the guilty with the rewards of heaven for those who lead a life of virtue

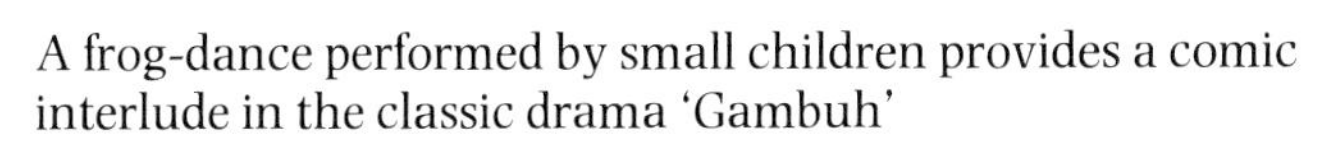

A frog-dance performed by small children provides a comic interlude in the classic drama 'Gambuh'

OPPOSITE In the trance-dance which enacts the battle between Barong and Rangda, men armed with Kris daggers rush to the defence of Barong, but the witch casts a spell which makes them turn their daggers back on themselves

ABOVE Offerings for the gods and spirits should conform to the particular nature of the festival day. Each day of the week has its own colour, which governs the choice of flowers, and a number, which dictates the number of units in the offering

OPPOSITE For the once-in-a-lifetime temple festival of 'Eka Dasa Rudra' one village contributed this offering made entirely of rice pastry. Some 10 feet in height, it represents Meru, the cosmic mountain which stands at the heart of the Hindu universe. The face in the centre belongs to Bhoma, Son of the Earth

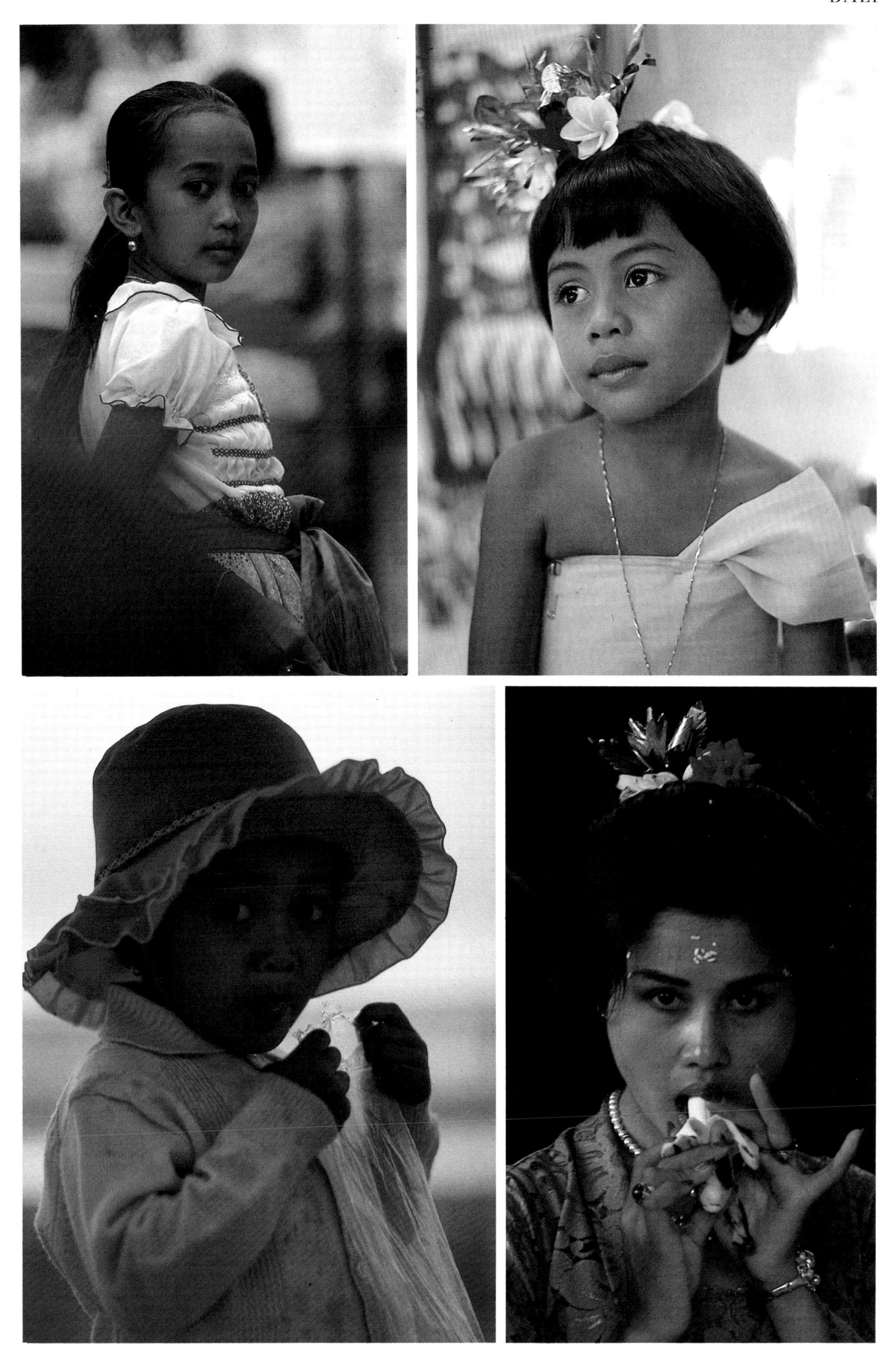

LEFT An offering at Besakih uses mirrors and a mask surrounded by cakes of rice

A young princess in the palace of Kerambitan receives holy water from a priest during a ceremony marking her coming of age. At the beginning of her first menstruation a Balinese girl of noble birth is declared 'sebel', unclean, and kept in seclusion until a day chosen by the priest as auspicious for her purification. It is a solemn occasion, celebrated by every member of her family, and her father and sister join their prayers to those of the priest

ABOVE The tower for the cremation of Tjokorde Agung, prince of Ubud village, in January 1979

OPPOSITE The tower for the cremation of Tjokorde Agung's brother in August 1976

In a Balinese cremation ceremony, thousands of pounds worth of superb art-work disappears in flames in a matter of minutes. The purpose is to provide a grand send-off for the soul of the dead man, so that it may reach the higher world and be free for reincarnation into a better being

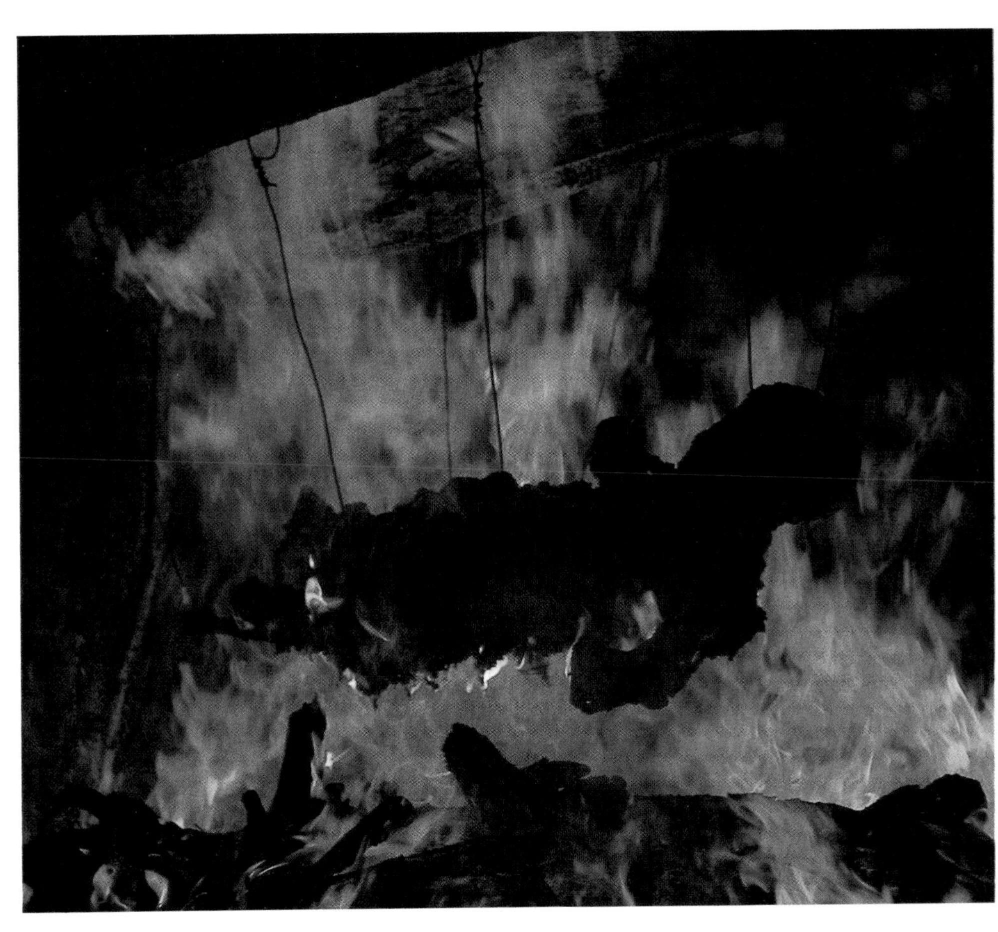

The corpse of Tjokorde Agung hanging from wires beneath its bull sarcophagus, and BELOW the high priest, Pedanda Dawan, chanting the holy mantras during the cremation

OPPOSITE Immolation of Bhoma, Son of the Earth, at the base of Tjokorde Agung's tower

In the temple courtyard of his palace in Peliatan, Anak Agung Gede Mandra teaches the most delicate and feminine of Balinese dances, the Legong. His pupils are young girls aged between 5 and 10, and he guides them physically, often violently, through the vigorous and dramatic gestures of the dance

OPPOSITE The family shrine has been adorned with lamaks, finely decorated strips of palm leaf, and the young dancers prepare to receive a sprinkling of holy water before they begin a Legong performance

ABOVE Oleg Tambulilingan is a dance depicting two bumble-bees flirting in a garden. Often performed as a prelude to the Legong, at its best it is a dance of extraordinary sensuality

OPPOSITE AND OVERLEAF Tightly bound from hand to foot in gold brocade, with a head-dress of beaten gold and frangipani flowers, the divine nymph of the Legong is a startled and startling figure. With flashing eyes and quivering fingers she stands rooted to the spot as if in trance. Suddenly she darts forward and begins to circle the temple courtyard, weaving this way and that, an arm rigidly outstretched, her eyes staring fixedly ahead of her. She never smiles, maintaining from start to finish an expression of studied seriousness

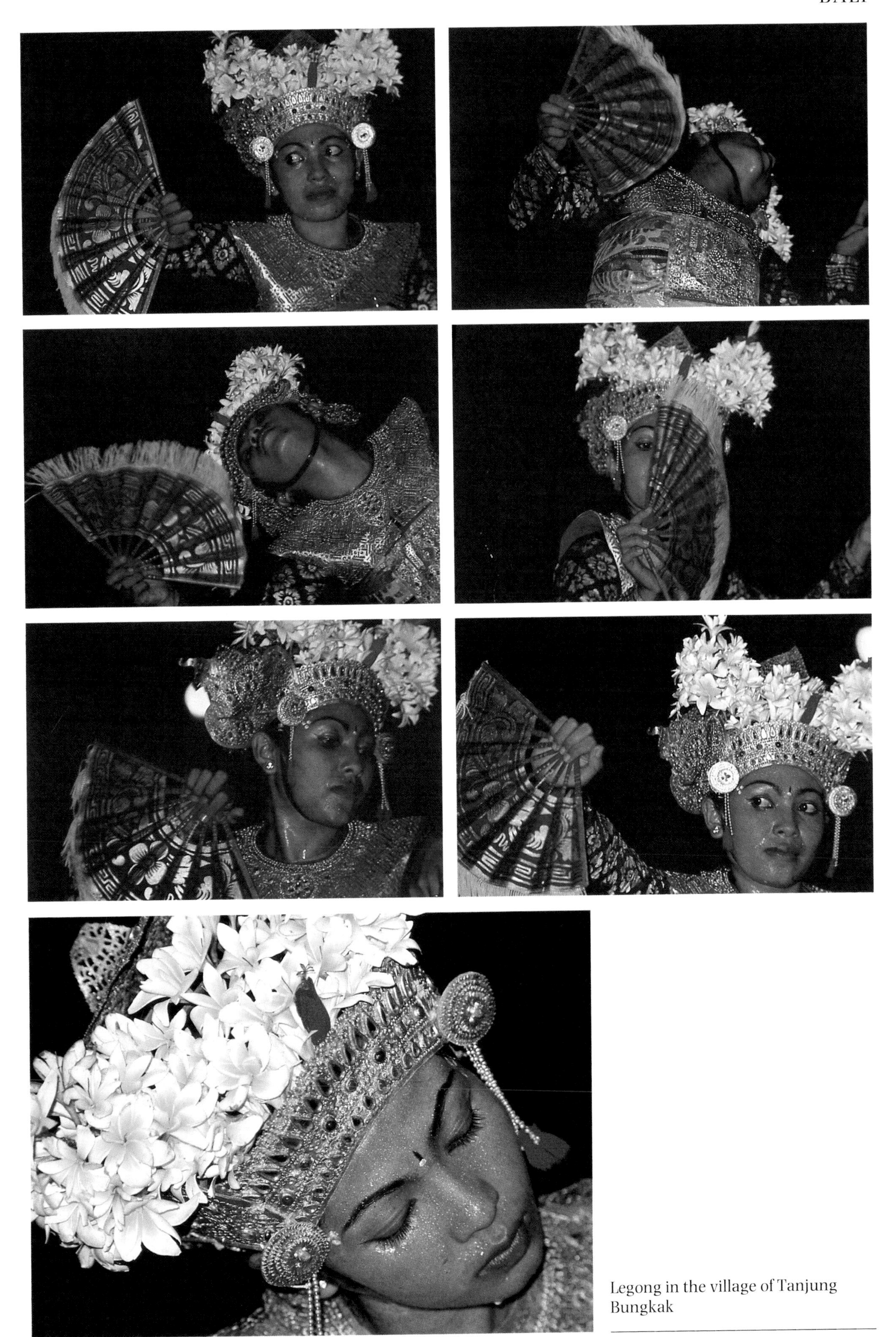

Legong in the village of Tanjung Bungkak

JAVA
'Land of the Cosmic Mountain'

Java is separated from Bali by a strip of water just two miles wide, and it might be supposed that the two islands would be very similar. In fact they are strikingly different. They have different languages, different religions – Java is Muslim – and the people have different temperaments. In her book *Art in Indonesia* Claire Holt points out that their dances too are surprisingly dissimilar:

> 'The Balinese is a startling and startled figure. Every part of his body is taut. His tense face, with wide-open eyes staring intently at an apparition visible only to himself, is like an erratic thunder-cloud cut by lightning. After an outburst of a few sudden swaggering steps forward the figure stops as abruptly as it had started.
>
> 'The forceful Javanese dancer projects no such hypnotic and startling intensity. It is the very expansiveness and stately, regular rhythm of his gestures that make him an unrelenting force, impersonal, impassive. Compared with the sudden outbursts of the hypertense Balinese dancer, the controlled poise of his Javanese counterpart seems an epitome of relentless steadiness.
>
> 'The feminine dances of the Javanese [serimpi] and Balinese [legong] offer even stronger contrasts. The dance of the serimpi, embellished by the unfolding, falling and fluttering of their dance scarves is stately and restrained. The glance of the dancer is constantly lowered, lending her performance a concentrated inwardness. At her fastest, a serimpi glides tiptoe over the floor in tiny, even steps, with one of her extended scarf-ends fluttering at her side.
>
> 'In contrast, the lithe bodies of the Balinese legong are propelled in rapid staccato rhythms. Instead of the delicate tip-toeing of the serimpi, the legong moves in a dust-raising lateral shuffle which sends her scooting in one direction and then in another.'

In Java, dances tend to be slow and languorous: 'a good dancer while executing serimpi feels no joy or exuberance; in its mood is none of the brilliance of the sun, but rather the radiance of the full moon, half-hidden by clouds'.

Sheltered within the elegant seclusion of the Kratons, the Sultan's palaces of Jogjakarta and Surakarta, dancing masters of the courts continue to instruct their pupils as they have done for centuries. It was here that the dances of India, originally a ritual offering to the god Shiva, were combined with the

Detail of relief carving on the west wall of Borobudur temple. Height: *c*. 20 cm

fertility rites of the native Javanese and transformed over the years into the pure and serene classical dances performed today – the Serimpi and the Bedoyo. The Serimpi is a stylised combat between two pairs of girls, its Hindu origins now completely disguised within a story from Islam. Bedoyo is a dance of gently flowing movements performed by nine girls in the costumes of brides, and it still maintains a spirit of ritual and mysticism. As with the dances of India, even the minutest gesture, however slow, is governed by strict rules, but here the language has been greatly simplified, and there is a restraint, more characteristic of Islamic puritanism than of Hindu expressiveness.

The Indian poet Rabindranath Tagore, visiting Java, wrote, 'I see India everywhere, but I do not recognise it.' The influence of India on the cultural life of Java was profound, but whether it be music and dancing, sculpture or temple building, the Indian model was adapted to suit Javanese taste, often being grafted on to an existing art form of the native people. Thus, in the case of the famous Javanese shadow puppets, a ritual performance based on the animistic belief that shadows were the manifestations of ancestral spirits became one of the media for enacting the old Hindu epics, the Ramayana and the Mahabharata. The puppets had so firm a hold on the Javanese imagination that they offered a ready channel through which the new ideas could pass and be assimilated. In the same way they are sometimes used today to tell a Christian story, even to support a government programme such as birth control. But no matter what the message may be or where the performance takes place, the shadow play maintains an aura of magic and ritual, and the 'dalang' or puppeteer never fails to make offerings of rice and flowers, before he begins.

> 'Sometimes he holds a few of the puppets over the rising smoke of incense and with an incantation propitiates the magically potent personages they embody: bringing down to earth deities and semi-divine beings in name and image is not free from danger.'

Shadow puppets are made from buffalo hide, brightly painted, and with a spine of horn. They come in a vast range of shapes and sizes, representing kings and princesses, clowns, ogres and demons – in all, a staggeringly varied population of more than 300 characters. Each individual puppet is instantly recognised by the audience the moment its shadow is cast on the screen by the flickering light of an oil lamp. Apart from manipulating the puppets, the dalang also directs the gamelan orchestra, narrates the story, and provides voices for every character, an astonishing virtuoso performance which he maintains throughout the night.

India's influence on Java probably began as early as the second century AD with the arrival of trading ships, and became stronger with the growth of great centres of learning within India itself under the Pallava and Gupta dynasties. With the merchants came missionaries and the Hindu faith, together with Buddhism at a time when that religion was actually in decline in the country of its birth. They brought with them their knowledge and skills in temple-building and sculpture, both in the round and in the form of relief carvings on temple walls, and they brought also the concept of a divine ruler. It was not a case of colonisation, but a gradual process by which Indian ideas were assimilated quite voluntarily and adapted to the needs of the Javanese people.

The 6000-foot high plateau of Dieng is a mysterious region of mist and cloud and bubbling volcanic springs. From early times it has been regarded as sacred, the 'Abode of the Gods', the Mount Olympus of Central Java. Here the people built shrines to contain the bones of their dead and to honour the spirits of the departed. With the coming of Hinduism, Dieng was elected the dwelling place of Shiva, God of Destruction, a natural choice in this area of intense volcanic activity, and in place of their ancestors the people now dedicated their temples to him. The plateau grew to be a holy centre of pilgrimage, a flourishing city of temples and hermitages, and it is here that we can find today a group of the earliest of Javanese temple-shrines in the Indian style. Built during the eighth century, they are tiny but beautifully proportioned, and already they show the grace and restrained elegance which were to make Javanese architecture outstanding throughout Asia.

The 200 years which followed was a period of intense activity among sculptors and temple-builders in all parts of central Java, truly a golden age for art of every kind. Its crowning achievement was Borobudur – a colossal man-made cosmic mountain, one of the most impressive creations of mankind – erected by the Sailendra dynasty, the 'Lords of the Mountain', several hundred years before the great cathedrals of Western Europe, and 300 years before Cambodia's celebrated Angkor Wat. Built with more than two million cubic feet of stone, it is the world's largest stupa (a form of stylised burial mound) and the largest ancient monument in the southern hemisphere.

Borobudur takes the form of a giant Buddhist prayer symbol, the mandala, constructed to look like Mount Meru of Hindu mythology. It combines the circle (heaven), the square (earth) and the stupa into one coherent whole, a symbol of the universe. The walls and balustrades of the lower terraces are adorned with a profusion of elaborately carved bas-reliefs: a series of 1450 panels tells the story of Buddha's life, from his descent from Tushita heaven to his achievement of Supreme Knowledge and entry to Nirvana, whilst another series of 1212 panels are purely decorative and treated as individual reliefs.

Entering the monument, the pilgrim is symbolically swallowed by the Kala monster, devourer of time, vividly portrayed over the doorway. Turning left he begins to circle the monument, always keeping the wall reliefs to his right. As he ascends, terrace by terrace, he receives new spiritual strength as the events depicted on the reliefs gradually lead him away from the earthly existence towards the Buddhist goal of Nirvana, nothingness, represented on Borobudur by a pattern of seventy-two bell-shaped 'dagobas' on the circular upper terraces, each one containing a statue of the Buddha but totally devoid of decoration. It is a region of abstraction, of pure shape.

To a Buddhist, the world we live in is a world of illusion, subject to constant change and governed by 'Karma', the Law of Cause and Effect. When a man dies, the Karma he has acquired in life will decide the nature of his next incarnation, and he will be reborn again and again in the endless cycle of transmigration. The only way to break the cycle is to gain the spiritual knowledge formulated by Buddha in the 'Four Noble Truths' and the 'Eightfold Path', and only then may he attain Nirvana.

The operation of the Law of Cause and Effect is illustrated at Borobudur by a series of 160 panels around the wall of the base. Hitherto these were obscured by stonework, added long ago to support the lower terraces, but the recent programme of restoration has brought them to light once again. Here, in vigorous and beautiful carving, are depicted the rewards of good deeds and the punishments for bad, cautionary tales for the pilgrim of the day, and for us, more than a thousand years later, a fascinating picture of daily life in Java as it was then.

Today more than 90 per cent of Javanese are Muslims, but each year, on Waisak day, Borobudur becomes once more a centre of Buddhist pilgrimage. In celebration of the day on which the Buddha received enlightenment (the same day of the year commemorates his birth, death, and attainment of Nirvana) monks converge on Borobudur from all parts of Buddhist Asia – Sri Lanka, Thailand, Burma, the countries of the Himalayas, and Japan. It is a great occasion, but not purely a Buddhist one, and Waisak has become a festive event for everyone, Buddhist and Muslim alike. There are even traces of the old animism, in the dances performed as entertainment for the visitors. Here certainly Rabindranath Tagore would see India but not recognise it.

No one knows how long Borobudur remained in

active use, but we may be sure that by the start of the thirteenth century the days of its glory were over. This was the beginning of a brief but spectacular period in Java's history during which Gajah Mada, a great general of the Hindu Majapahit dynasty, succeeded in uniting the far-flung islands of Indonesia from Sumatra in the west, through Malaya and Borneo, as far as the Moluccas in the east. It was also the time when Islam was beginning to make its presence felt.

In 1292 Marco Polo visited Indonesia:

> '... [Java] is the biggest island in the world, having a circumference of more than 3000 miles. The people are idolaters ruled by a powerful monarch and paying no tribute to anyone on earth. It is a very rich island, producing pepper, nutmegs, spikenard, galingale, cubebs and cloves. . . . It is visited by great numbers of ships and merchants who buy a great range of merchandise, reaping handsome profits and rich returns. The quantity of treasure in the island is beyond all computation.... You must know that the people of Ferlec [north-west Sumatra] used all to be idolaters, but owing to contact with Saracen merchants, who continually resort here in their ships, they have all been converted to the law of Mahomet.'

By the end of the sixteenth century, Islam had spread from Sumatra and was firmly established throughout Java. In the past, it had conquered by force of arms, but in Java the process of conversion was accomplished by little more violence than the beheading of the Borobudur Buddhas by Muslim vandals – the Koran forbids the worship of idols.

At that time the people were little better than slaves, in thrall to a feudal overlord who could order them to do whatever he wished – a state of affairs which made possible the building of great temples but did not always endear a ruler to his subjects. It is easy to imagine the appeal of the egalitarian code of Islam, under which all men are regarded as equal in the eyes of Allah. The Hindu concept of a divine ruler was replaced by the idea that Sultans became saints after their death and could then be worshipped as such. Signal towers were converted into minarets, meeting halls became the palaces of the Sultanate.

But these changes were essentially superficial – the Sultans continued to exercise the power they had previously enjoyed as rajahs, and the ancient practice of spirit worship continued to control the lives of the people, just as it had done during the great Hindu dynasties of previous years. It was the mystical aspect of Islam, 'sufism', rather than the dogma, which gained acceptance, and this was blended with elements of earlier religions – animism, ancestor-worship, Hinduism and Buddhism – to form a new faith, 'Agama Jawa', the uniquely Javanese form of Islam which one finds throughout Indonesia today.

In the new religion there was no place for Borobudur – its superb representations of the Buddha and the events of his life were anathema to the crusading Muslims. Gradually the temple was swallowed up by jungle and forgotten, and it was not until the early nineteenth century that steps were taken to rescue it from oblivion. Java was then under British rule and the Governor, Stamford Raffles, took an interest in the temple and began the mighty task of restoration which continues to this day.

For Borobudur, restoration is not simply a matter of cosmetic surgery, of clearing foliage and repairing stonework. The main problem is that the core is no longer able to support the monument. Borobudur was built around a natural hill in a region of torrential rains, and constant seepage of rainwater during ten centuries gradually washed away the core material. Lacking support, the upper levels of the temple began to settle, causing the terraces to sag and the walls to lean outwards. Raffles could do little to tackle this basic problem. Van Erp, a Dutch archaeologist working early this century, did much to restore the superstructure, but even he had not the resources to ensure that the monument would not eventually collapse.

In 1955 the Indonesian Government asked

Unesco for assistance, and a detailed survey of the monument was carried out. It was decided that the only way to save Borobudur was to dismantle it and then rebuild it on a foundation of reinforced concrete, and with a drainage system which would prevent further seepage through the stonework. The work began in 1971, and restoration is expected to be completed by 1982. One million stone blocks must be removed and individually classified so that they may be reassembled in the correct position, a task only possible with the aid of computers. Damaged blocks must be replaced by new ones, carefully cut to size. Blocks carrying relief carvings must be cleaned of corrosive chemicals and lichens, and treated to prevent future growths. The severed heads of more than sixty Buddha statues must be reunited with their bodies – another job for the computer, which is able to analyse the break of a neck and match it to a similar contour on the neck of a torso. More than a thousand years ago, Borobudur was built by peasant labour over a period of about thirty years. Today, again with peasant labour, it is being dismantled and rebuilt all over again. This time some 600 people are involved, over a period of ten years. When they have finished, the temple should look very much as it did in the ninth century, but now it will have a solid centre. Theoretically, it should last for ever.

ABOVE A gallery in the Kraton, the Sultan's palace in Jogjakarta, central Java

OPPOSITE Ploughing a rice paddy near Borobudur

A lesson in classical dancing is given in the Kraton every weekend, attended by people from many different walks of life who are attracted by a discipline and control which can produce a serenity like that of meditation

OPPOSITE The Dance of Great Birds tells a story of Islam, but the girls ride the birds as Vishnu rides the Garuda in Hindu mythology. It is one of many examples in Indonesia of Islam combining with the earlier arts of Hinduism to create something new and unique to this country

The celebrated shadow puppets of Java have their origins in the ancient belief that shadows are the manifestations of ancestral spirits. Today they tell stories which came from India – the great epics Ramayana and Mahabharata – but they still maintain an aura of magic, and the puppeteer still makes an offering to the spirits before he begins the play

OPPOSITE In the Kraton of Jogjakarta craftsmen among the court attendants work on a new set of shadow puppets, cutting the designs from buffalo hide and fixing them to a spine of horn. They use no stencil, but rely on memory to reproduce the precise features of more than 300 different characters

OVERLEAF The Buddhist temple of Borobudur in central Java

The Buddhist temple of Borobudur in central Java is a colossal man-made cosmic mountain, the largest ancient monument in the southern hemisphere. With more than 2 million cubic feet of stone, it was built by peasant labour over a period of 30 years finishing around AD 800, the crowning glory of the Sailendra dynasty. Today, more than 90 per cent of Javanese are Muslims and the temple is no longer in general use. But once a year, on the Buddha's birthday, Borobudur becomes again a centre of Buddhist pilgrimage when monks from many different parts of Asia converge on the temple to celebrate the festival of Waisak

One of the 72 Buddha images concealed in the bell-shaped 'dagobas' on the circular upper terraces of Borobudur. There are no decorative panels in this part of the temple – it is a region of abstract shape, a representation of nothingness: the Buddhist Nirvana

The walls and balustrades of Borobudur are adorned with a profusion of beautifully carved relief panels. A series of nearly 1500 tell the story of Buddha's life, while others are used purely as decoration. These, on the lowest level, are concerned with 'Karma', the Law of Cause and Effect. For centuries they were hidden by stonework built to strengthen the monument, but the recent programme of restoration has once more exposed them to the light of day

OVERLEAF Decorative panels on Borobudur. 1460 panels encircling the temple tell the story of Buddha's life, from his descent from Tushita heaven to his achievement of Supreme Knowledge and entry to Nirvana. They are so arranged that the pilgrim circles the temple, keeping them always to his right. Other panels offer many glimpses of life at the time of the Sailendras – for instance a ship of the kind that must have plied between Java and the trading ports of 8th-century India

The restoration of Borobudur is the most complex task of its kind ever undertaken. It is being dismantled, a section at a time, and rebuilt on foundations of reinforced concrete. A million stone blocks must be removed and individually classified so that they can be reassembled in the correct position. Damaged blocks must be replaced by new ones, and those with relief carvings must be cleansed of lichens and corrosive chemicals. Some 500 Buddhas must be individually cared for, and severed heads reunited with their bodies

In marked contrast to the Balinese legong, the feminine dances of Java are slow and languorous. There is none of the startled intensity of the Balinese, but instead a feeling of controlled inwardness and spiritual calm

ABOVE A student of the Bedoyo dance during a lesson in the Kraton

OPPOSITE A sacred dance performed at Mendut temple to an audience of Buddhist monks attending the Waisak festival

ABOVE The 10th-century Hindu temple of Prambanan towers majestically above the rice fields of central Java. Almost 50 metres high, it was for 1000 years the tallest building in the country

OPPOSITE A dancer at Prambanan carries a kris, a weapon believed to contain the magical power of ancestor-spirits. It is said that a shaman, through trance, can speak with the spirit of a particular kris and learn its past history

In the courtyard of Prambanan temple, girls from Jogjakarta perform the gently flowing movements of Bedoyo, a dance nurtured within the courts of Sultans but originating in the temple dances of India more than 1000 years ago

OPPOSITE Bima temple on Dieng plateau, 'Abode of the Gods', one of the earliest temples in Java to show the influence of India. It is dedicated to Shiva – in this volcanic region it is natural that the people should have chosen as their chief deity the God of Destruction

In central Java a man riding a hobby-horse believes himself possessed by a horse-spirit. He is in powerful trance, unable to feel pain as he gallops through fire. Everything in his behaviour is horse-like. He will drink water from a bucket and tear with his teeth at the fibres of an unhusked coconut. Needles penetrate his cheeks, but still he appears to feel no pain

ABOVE Head of the Bodhisattva Manjushri, from Plaosan temple, central Java, 2nd half of the 9th century. Height 33.5 cm

OPPOSITE Near Jogjakarta. The volcano Mt Merapi is in the background

INDIA
'The Story of Rama'

Among the cultural riches bestowed by India on the lands of South-east Asia, one particular work of art stands out ahead of all others: 'Ramayana'. This ancient story of heroism and villainy was able to take so firm a hold on the imagination of the people that now, 2000 years later, it still maintains a universal popularity. Wherever one goes in South-east Asia one finds the Ramayana – in carvings on temple walls, drawings on old palm-leaf manuscripts, in magical shadow-plays and classical dance-dramas. The 'Khon' dance of Thailand, the ritualistic 'Kechak' monkey-dance of Bali, the serene Ramayana Ballet of Java – each of them takes the same story as its source material, though the manner of presentation can be strikingly different from one country to another.

Ramayana, 'The Story of Rama', was written down by the Indian poet Valmiki some 200 years before the Christian era. With more than 24,000 verses of Sanskrit filling seven volumes and with a cast of hundreds, it has the dimensions of an epic, but the story is essentially a simple one, easily understood and remembered by young and old alike. Rama, the princely incarnation of the Hindu god Vishnu, wins the hand of a beautiful young princess, Sita, by breaking the great bow of Shiva. But his happiness is short-lived: his step-mother, wishing to place her own son on the throne of the Kingdom of Ayodya, pleads with the King to grant her a wish. When he agrees she demands that Rama be banished for fourteen years. Amid great sorrow, Rama leaves the palace and, with Sita and his loyal brother Lakshmana, enters the forest. Ravana, the evil King of Lanka, desires to have Sita for himself, and he sends a golden deer to entice Rama and Lakshmana deeper into the forest, leaving Sita unprotected. When they have gone, Ravana abducts the girl and flies off with her to his palace. After many adventures, and with the aid of an army of monkeys led by their general, Hanuman, Rama succeeds in reaching the palace of Lanka. There is a mighty battle, Ravana is killed by a magic arrow from Rama's bow, and Sita is rescued. Triumphantly the heroes return to Ayodya, where the step-brother, Bharata, gladly gives up the throne he has guarded during the years of exile, and Rama is crowned King.

In South-east Asia it is this basic story which is enacted over and over again, with particular emphasis on the abduction of Sita and her eventual rescue. The detailed ramifications of the plot are

Early morning in the desert of Rajasthan near the fortress city of Jaiselmer

ignored. But in India the epic tale has survived in its entirety, and every year, in October and November, it is played out, scene by scene, from start to finish, with two great festivals commemorating the moments of triumph in the story. Dussehra celebrates the ten-day battle which culminates in the death of Ravana, whilst Diwali, the Festival of Lights, marks the royal homecoming three weeks later.

In different parts of the country, Dussehra takes many different forms. In the foothills of the Himalayas, villagers from neighbouring valleys converge in long processions on the valley of Kulu, bringing with them images of their gods mounted on palanquins. The purpose of their pilgrimage is to pay homage to a tiny golden statue of Rama, only two inches high, but the most sacred object they know. At the opposite extreme are the giant images of Ravana and his two brothers which stand at the heart of the celebrations in Delhi. Constructed of bamboo and coloured paper, stuffed with home-made fireworks, and towering 100 feet above the ground, they provide a thrilling climax to the story, as they are set on fire and rapidly disintegrate in a shower of sparks and a great cloud of smoke. Rama has vanquished the Demon King; Good has triumphed over Evil. Everyone goes home to bed well pleased.

Whilst Delhi offers perhaps the greatest spectacle, it is to the holy city of Benares that one must go for the best traditional enactment of the Ramayana. It uses the world's largest theatre – the great Ramlila parade ground of Ramnagar fort, home of the Maharajah of Benares, which faces the city across the broad reach of the sacred Ganges river. A considerable area of countryside is laid out to represent the actual territory – Ayodya, Lanka, the forest – over which the action of the drama unfolds. In place of the Western device of a single stage with changes of scenery, there are numerous stages, each one representing a particular location – a hermitage in the forest perhaps, or the palace of the Demon King. When one scene comes to an end the complete audience, which may be as many as half a million people, moves away towards the stage where the next scene is ready to begin. Ahead of them goes the Maharajah, the patron of the drama, riding an elephant magnificently adorned for the occasion, and accompanied by a great cry from the crowd – 'Ha Ha Maha Deva', 'Hail, Hail, Lord Shiva'. To the people of Benares, the Maharajah is, like Rama, an incarnation of one of their great deities.

During each of the thirty days spanning Dussehra, people converge on Ramnagar in their thousands, and among them are many Sadhus, holy men, who travel vast distances to be present at what is, for them, not an entertainment but an act of worship. They have come to see their gods become manifest in human form. When Rama mounts the stage they are looking not at an actor, but at Vishnu himself. As the god begins to speak, in a slow, monosyllabic and declamatory manner, so that his words carry to everyone present, an extraordinary hush settles on the gigantic crowd. Among half a million people there is no movement, no murmur to break the spell.

The actors at Ramnagar are of two kinds. Mortal beings – kings and queens, demons, birds, monkeys, politicians – are played by village people, well known to many of the audience. Hanuman may be the local butcher, King Dasaratha the local blacksmith. In this way a close rapport is established between the actor and his public. He plays for only one month of the year, but always in the same role, and he quickly becomes identified with that part. Hanuman will be addressed as Hanuman throughout the year, and nobody will remember his real name any more.

Godlike characters – Rama, Sita, Lakshmana – are played by boys of between six and fourteen years of age. For three months the boys are taken away from their parents and kept in an ashram, a lonely place of seclusion where they are looked after by the director of the play. During this period they are treated as the gods they are to represent and each day the village people bring them garlands of flowers to drape across their shoulders, and offerings of food and money. When the first day of the festival arrives, the boys endure an elaborate make-up lasting three or four hours as their faces are decorated with paint and intricate patterns of brightly coloured sequins. During this ordeal, and at all times throughout the festival, they must behave in a serious and dignified manner, as befits a god.

In Benares, the climax of the festivities comes not with the death of Ravana, as in Delhi, but later in the story, at the point where Rama, Sita and Lakshmana return home to Ayodya. After fourteen years in exile, they are joyfully reunited with the brothers they had left behind, and this scene is enacted amid a wave of emotion and religious ecstasy bordering on hysteria. It lasts, in all, just four minutes – in the words of a local devotee, 'The Greatest Show on Earth and of the shortest duration!'

At the time of Dussehra the people of eastern India hold a different festival, 'Durga Puja'. Benares is on the dividing line between east and west, and so is able to enjoy the best of both: here the two celebrations take place together. Durga is the 'terrible' form of the Great Goddess, the consort of Shiva, and she represents divine energy. Her purpose is to maintain the peace of the world by opposing the forces of disruption, and the festival commemorates the day she slew the buffalo-headed demon Mahishasura. Like Dussehra it is a celebration of the victory of good over evil.

On the day of Durga Puja, enormous images of the goddess are carried through the streets of the city amid a wild cacophony of rattling drums and screaming trumpets, and the cries of half a million excited spectators. On reaching the Ganges, the images are loaded on to houseboats and carried out to midstream. As the sun disappears behind the palaces and minarets which line the river bank, the Durgas are cast into the holy waters to drift away into the gathering gloom.

The continuing popularity of the Ramayana in India owes much to the efforts of one man – Tulsi Das – who, early in the sixteenth century, translated the epic poem from the original Sanskrit into the vernacular Hindi. As a memorial to his gargantuan achievement, there is now a temple in Benares containing the whole of Tulsi's Ramayana engraved on marble slabs around the walls. Sanskrit is no longer spoken in India, but near the southern tip of the country, in the state of Kerala, Sanskrit theatre still survives in the form of an ancient dance-drama called Kutiyattam, and it still relies on the Valmiki Ramayana for its basic material. Kutiyattam has much in common with the better-known Kathakali which it may have inspired. Great use is made of grotesquely exaggerated make-up, huge headdresses, like crowns with haloes, and brightly coloured voluminous costumes. Both dance forms are kept alive today by a celebrated Academy of Arts, founded fifty years ago by the poet Vallathol in the small town of Cheruthuruthi. Here the students, mainly boys, struggle to master an immense vocabulary of gestures – movement of eyes, arms, hands, feet, facial expressions – all of which must be precisely synchronised and used in a disciplined manner to convey the emotions and actions of the story. The hand-gestures, 'mudras', are particularly difficult to learn: a characteristic of Indian dance in general, in Kathakali they are the principal means of expression. A sequence of mudras, finely executed, is like a miniature dance of the fingers, visually pleasing and, at the same time, a way of vividly underlining the meaning of the song they accompany. There is a mudra for every word, and the trained Kathakali dancer must have at least 500 of them at his command.

Training for the dance is long and arduous. The course lasts for eight to twelve years, and each day begins at 3.30 in the morning with a painful massage, a much-hated feature of the training. The young boys, naked but for a scanty loincloth, are covered with palm oil and stretched out on the stone floor, whilst their teachers, standing over them, pummel their muscles with the soles of their feet. The purpose is to provoke an awareness of each separate part of the body so that every joint, every nerve and every muscle may later be controlled and called into play for dance movement.

It was during the 'Golden Age of Sanskrit', between AD 400 and 1000, that Indian culture took root in the soil of South-east Asian countries, and a form of theatre similar to Kutiyattam must certainly have existed at that time. Yet, surprisingly, no trace of Sanskrit theatre has ever been found in South-east Asia, and it appears that the famous Bharata Natya Shastra, the ancient Sanskrit treatise on the techniques of dance and drama, was not among the imported literature. Apparently it was through public recitations in the vernacular languages of India, rather than the high courtly Sanskrit, that the great epics found their new audiences. For the prototype of Indian dance in South-east Asia we must look to the classical dance style of Bharata Natyam, the most completely preserved and most anciently documented of any surviving classic dance in the world.

Though once performed by men, Bharata Natyam is presented today only by women, in solo recitals lasting around two and a half hours. It is a dance of vertiginous speed requiring almost superhuman strength and stamina and the ability to express an astonishingly wide range of emotions. The dancer begins with a brilliant display of technical virtuosity, an explosion of movement. She bends and dips, whirls and leaps, and with stomping feet beats out a complex rhythm, which the tinkling bells around her feet make audible. In the middle of her programme come the 'Padas', songs of religious devotion, and it is in the way she conveys the various underlying meanings of these songs that a dancer may prove her artistry. Every word, phrase and sentence must first be conveyed with literal gestures and precise facial expressions. The dancer then proceeds to improvise, suggesting the various alternative ways in which the words of the song might be interpreted. In the sentence 'I worship you, oh my Lord Shiva', the word 'worship' implies the relationship between a devotee and his god, but it might equally describe the feelings of a young girl towards her lover. To portray this extra meaning, the dancer coyly flirts with her invisible Lord as if he were human.

Shiva, the creator and destroyer, may appear in many forms – a cobra, a bull, the River Ganges, or even the moon. In India every god has his particular attributes and characteristics and an unlimited number of manifestations, and all of these are available to the dancer for her interpretation. They provide her with a source of expressive symbolism which is inexhaustible.

Except among the most highly educated of city dwellers, neither Bharata Natyam nor Kathakali enjoy wide popularity in India today, but in Delhi an enterprising academy of dance has skilfully combined elements of these and other traditional dances to tell their own version of the Ramayana story, and it has proved highly successful. Each year throughout Dussehra they play to a nightly audience of some 3000 people. The dancing is of a high standard, and yet it is the story itself which finally ensures the success of the evening's entertainment. Once again the Ramayana demonstrates its capacity to hold an audience spellbound.

A dancer's performance is judged in terms of 'bhava' and 'rasa', ancient concepts still used in India to qualify artistic expression of all kinds. Rasa means feeling or flavour, and describes the major emotions – heroism, fear, love, terror, pathos, etc. – conveyed by the dance. Bhava, on the other hand, consists of acts and situations which evoke specific responses. When the bhavas of the dance are properly portrayed, the rasa appears as an overpowering aesthetic reaction from within the spectator, a state of religious ecstasy which, according to the Hindu, only true art can arouse.

There are many opinions as to the origins and true meaning of the Ramayana, and the reasons for its phenomenal success and popularity. 'Rama and Sita are so human, and they go through all the human difficulties, the ups and downs of life. They are our idols, so we try to become Rama and Sita' is how the

Maharajah of Benares expresses it. To Dr T. J. D. Singh, the President of an academy of music and drama in Benares, the power of the Ramayana lies in its ability to communicate on many different levels at one and the same time.

'According to Indian philosophy, man is a very complex being. He is not simply mind and body – a psychosomatic organism, as the psychologists put it. He is body and mind plus what we call "prana maya ghosh", the life principle, plus "bhodi", a higher consciousness than the ordinary mental consciousness, and finally the "anandama ghosh" or the "great spirit" itself. Ramayana succeeds in bringing out the importance of all of these levels.'

Dr Mehta, a medical practitioner in Benares and an authority on Indian theatre, sees the Ramayana in terms of psychological analogy.

'It is the good and bad in ourselves which are the characters of the Ramayana. Rama is the goodness of the human being – the soul – and Ravana is the ego. When the ego takes over, evil things like greed and jealousy and selfishness come up – these are the characters on the evil side. Good things like patience, friendship, giving of alms, non-violence – these are the characters on Rama's side. The devotion to god is represented in Sita, the consort of Rama, but the ego removes that devotion, and then you see there is evil all around. Thus the struggle goes on, but in the end the ego, Ravana, is killed, and devotion is brought back.'

Many people believe that the Ramayana refers to the coming to India of the Aryan race around 5000 BC and their conflict with the native Dravidians. But it appears that there really was a King Rama, at a much later time, and another king named Ravana, and it may have happened that a serious disagreement led to a great battle which became immortalised in folk tales and later formed the basis of Valmiki's epic poem. The solar dynasty of Rajasthan, whose descendants now live in the palaces of Jodhpur, Jaipur and Udaipur, actually claim Rama as their ancestor, and believe that the sacred lake of Pushkar once received a visit from Rama himself.

For the people of India as a whole, such considerations of authenticity are of only secondary importance. The Ramayana is, first and foremost, a religious work, the living credo of a people's faith, and throughout this land of great diversity it binds the Indian people together at the deepest levels. 'Rama' is the word Hindus hope to have on their lips when they die. It was Gandhi's last utterance.

ABOVE A chamber in the 16th-century lakeside palace of the Maharana of Udaipur

OPPOSITE Jaiselmer, Rajasthan

The sacred lake of Pushkar, a serenely beautiful oasis in the desert of Rajasthan. It is said that the god Brahma, the Creator, was passing this spot and let slip a lotus from his hand. Where the flower had fallen, water gushed forth, and from then on the lake of Pushkar has been revered as a holy place of Hindu pilgrimage.

According to tradition, the most auspicious moment for bathing in the lake is at the full moon of Kartik (November), and every year at this time the waters are ablaze with the vivid colours of saris and the bright sparkle of heavy silver bracelets

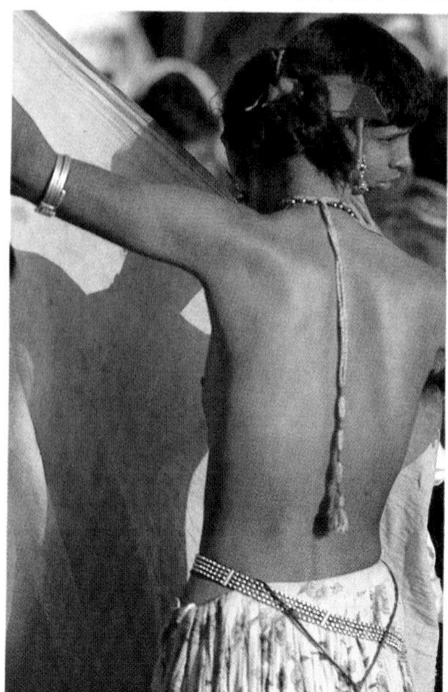

ABOVE A dancing nymph, carved in sandstone, decorates the pillar of a 15th-century temple in Jaiselmer, a remote desert city founded in 1156 as the 'Oasis of Jessel'

OPPOSITE In the mid-19th century the houses of wealthy merchants in Jaiselmer were fine palaces, decorated with superb carvings in stone as light and delicate as lace

OVERLEAF The annual Pushkar Fair

The Pushkar Fair is, first and foremost, a gigantic cattle market. At this one time in the year, the desert around the small oasis town becomes a sea of camels, stretching away into the distance until it disappears in a shimmering haze of mirage. From the beginning of November, whole families of desert people converge on Pushkar from all corners of Rajasthan, bringing with them the sum-total of their possessions, their camels, horses and cattle, and transforming this sleepy town into a bustling centre of commerce

डेन्टिस्ट
गुरबचनसिंह
सूचना:-
१ दांत के बनाने का ५/- यदि ज्यादा दांत
हे तो १ दांत का ४/- रुपये।

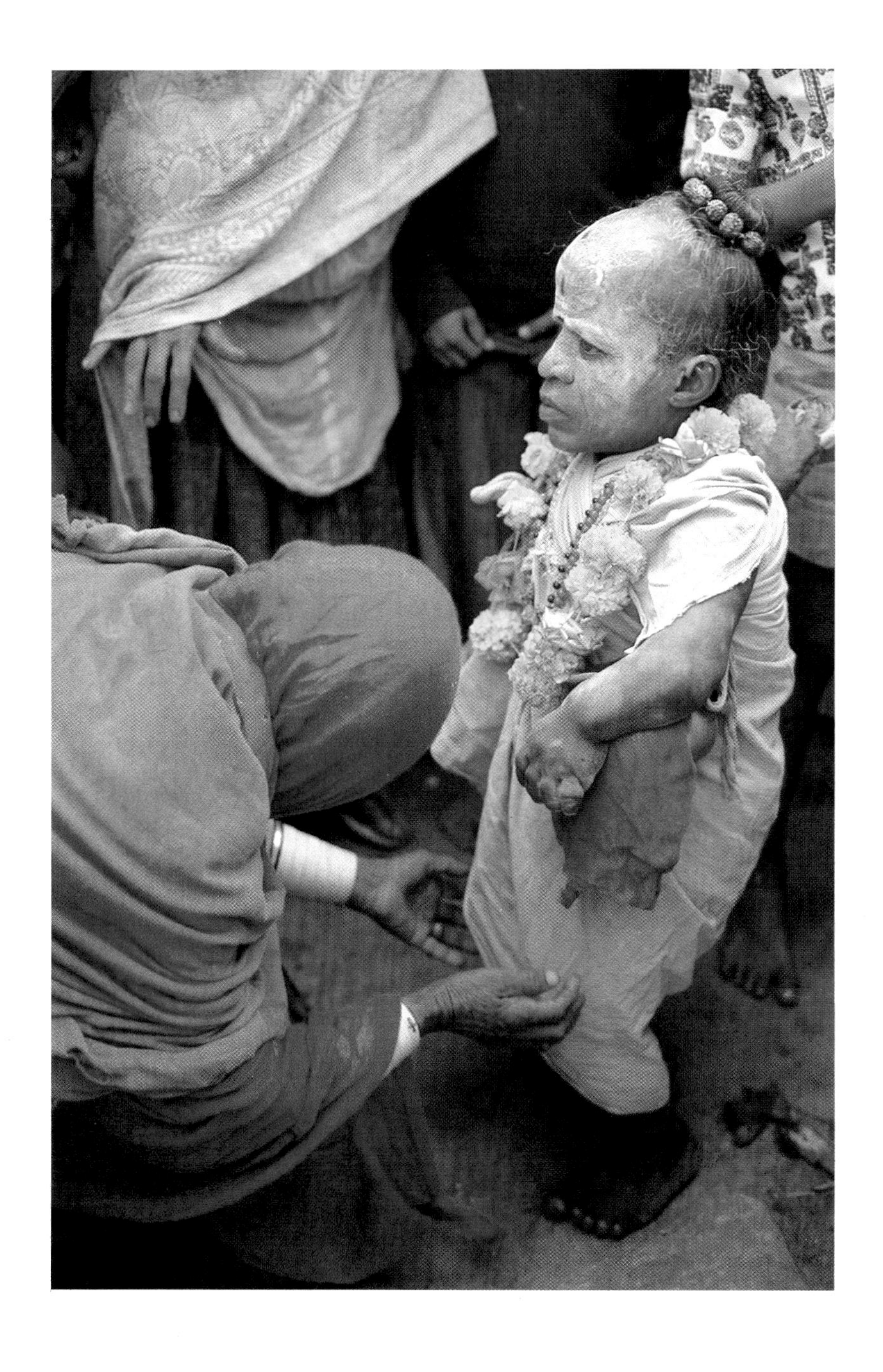

ABOVE In Pushkar town, a holy man is surrounded by devotees who kneel at his feet and grasp at the hem of his robe

OPPOSITE Three men of the desert pose for a photograph by the roadside, and a dentist squats on the pavement surrounded by the tools of his trade

OPPOSITE The Shore Temple at Mahabalipuram, south of Madras, was built in the 8th century by the kings of the Pallava dynasty

His skin glistening with coconut oil, a young student of Kathakali dancing receives an early-morning massage from his teacher.

After massage the boys practise the eye movements which are used to add meaning to the words of the drama. Expressions of the face are combined with movements of hands and feet in a complicated body-language which must be synchronised precisely with music and dialogue

Training for Kathakali is long and arduous. For at least 8 years, and for 13 hours a day, the boys must struggle to master an immense vocabulary of gestures – there are more than 500 for hands alone. Make-up is elaborate and grotesque, and it begins many hours before the start of the performance. The colours include green for godliness, black for evil and yellow for passivity. The eyes are usually red, having been inflamed by the insertion of plant seeds shortly before the actor takes the stage.

The most distinctive features of Kathakali are its voluminous costumes and enormous head-dresses. Kathakali is a revived art-form, and the dancers have sought to copy the appearance of their forebears as portrayed in paintings and carvings within the medieval temples of Kerala

Kumari Alarmel Valli performs Bharata Natyam, a temple dance of South India

OPPOSITE A lagoon on the southern coast of Kerala, a centre for the production of copra

ABOVE A girl of Rajasthan

RIGHT A man of Kulu valley in the Himalayas

ABOVE Sculpture on the wall of a temple at Mahabalipuram

OPPOSITE A life-size elephant carved from rock stands among the 7th-century temples of Mahabalipuram, south-east India

OVERLEAF The Ganges at Benares

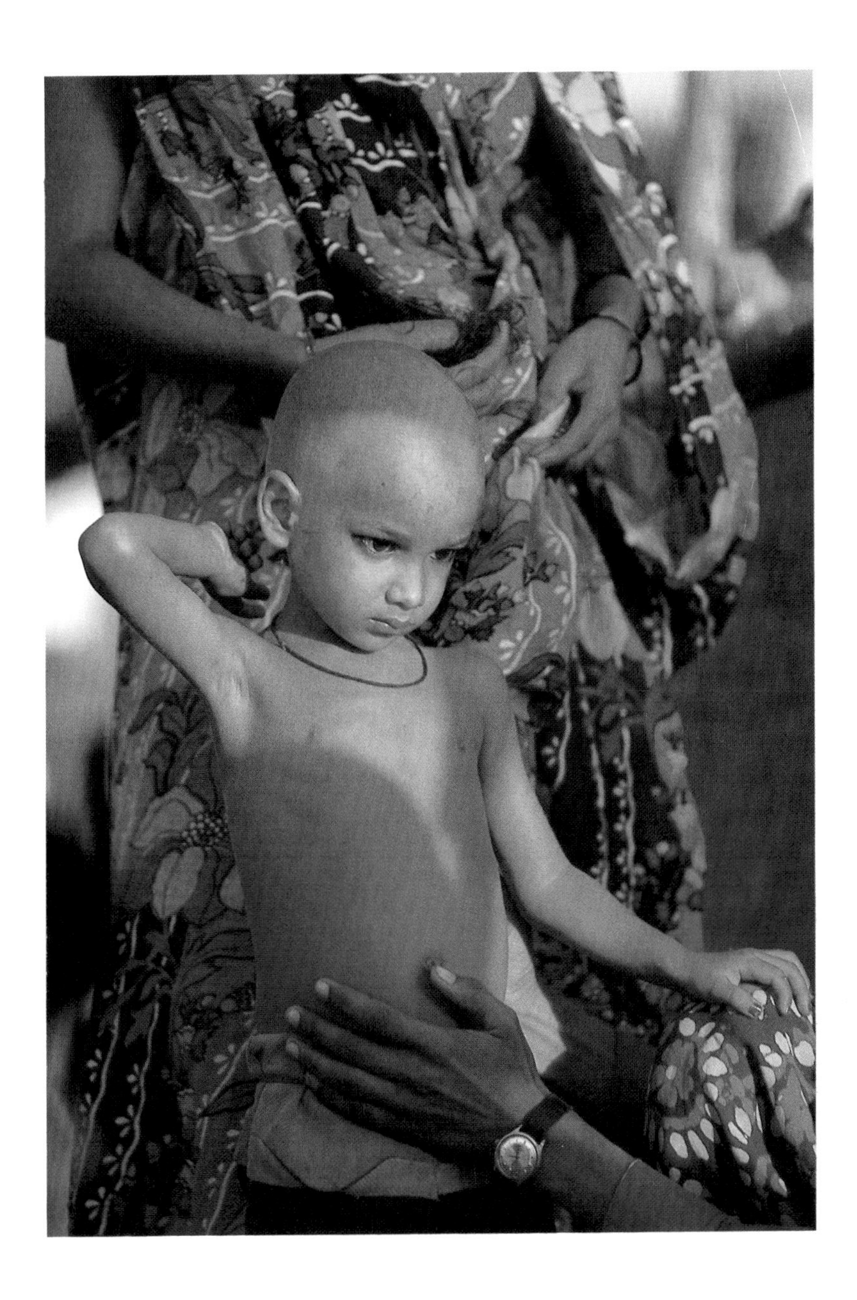

ABOVE After the ritual shaving of his head, a young boy stands with his parents beside the holy Ganges

OPPOSITE AND PREVIOUS PAGES Each day at sunrise the banks of the Ganges at Benares teem with life. Pilgrims from every corner of India come to bathe in the holy waters, for every Hindu hopes to visit Benares at least once in a lifetime, and if possible to die here in old age. For 3 miles, the river is lined with 'ghats', steps leading down the steep banks and into the water. Behind the ghats rise domes and minarets and the towers of derelict palaces.

When the Buddha came here some 2500 years ago, it was already an ancient city and a centre of pilgrimage. Its real age cannot be estimated, but Benares is probably the oldest living city in the world

The audience for one of the world's greatest theatrical events – the Ramlila of Ramnagar – approaches the open space where the drama is to take place

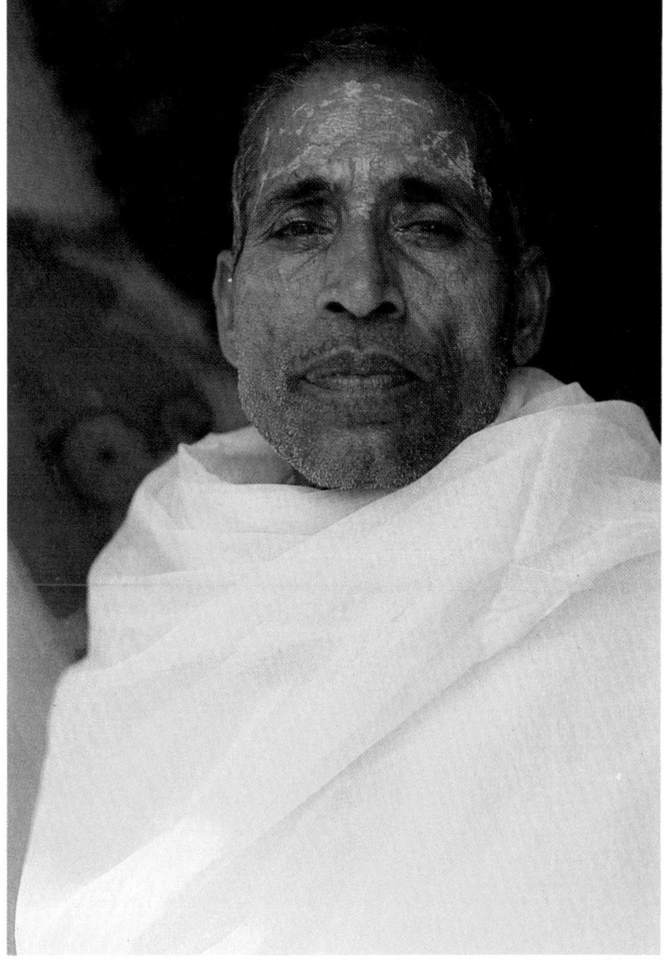

A woman at Ramnagar waits for the play to begin

'Hanuman', an actor in the drama, is at other times a dealer in saris, but all know him by his stage name and the yellow colour identifies him as a lifelong devotee of Hanuman, the monkey-god he portrays

A young boy, who portrays the god-prince Rama of the ancient epic poem 'Ramayana'. At Ramnagar, home of the Maharajah of Benares, the story is enacted scene by scene throughout the 30-day period which includes the annual Dussehra festival. The actors who play Rama, his wife and his brothers are boys between the ages of 6 and 14 who have been taken away from their parents and prepared for their sacred role within the holy precincts of an ashram

BELOW 'The greatest show on Earth and of the shortest duration!' In Benares the climax of the Ramayana story comes with the return of Rama, his wife and his brother after 14 years of exile. The scene lasts just 4 minutes

OVERLEAF An elephant carries the Maharajah through an excited crowd of half a million people. Before the play can begin, he must encircle the stage which bears the child actors, a mark of respect to the gods they represent

ABOVE In Delhi the climax of the Ramayana story comes with the death of the demon-king Ravana. Enormous effigies of the king and his brothers are burned amid a shower of sparks from home-made fireworks

OPPOSITE The dance of the bird Jatayu in the ballet version of the Ramayana, performed every year at the Ferozeshah Kotla ground in Delhi

OVERLEAF Throughout the Dussehra festival, the evening's drama ends with 'arti', a ritual of fire. At this point a great wave of emotion and religious fervour sweeps over the huge crowd of spectators: in the child actors revealed by the light of a flare they see before them the incarnation of their gods

CAMBODIA
'God-Kings of Angkor'

'It was as if a vegetation of stone had sprouted in thick impetuous profusion from the soil; fifty towers of different heights rising in tiers; fifty fantastic pineapples, grouped in a kind of bundle on a base as large as a town, almost hugging one another and forming a retinue to a central and more gigantic tower, some two hundred feet in height, which dominated them, its summit crowned with a golden lotus-flower. And from high in the air, those quadruple faces with which each of them was adorned gazed at the four cardinal points, gazed everywhere, with the same drooping eyelids, the same expression of ironical pity, the same smile. They affirmed, they repeated until it became a kind of obsession, the omnipresence of the god of Angkor.'

Those were the words of Pierre Loti, at the turn of this century, encountering for the first time the extraordinary jumble of stone towers which form the temple of Bayon at Angkor. At that time the Bayon was as romantic a sight as any lover of ruins could hope to find: almost completely engulfed by tropical jungle, its stonework entwined by the roots of giant fig trees, and high overhead, carved on every tower, gigantic heads, smiling enigmatically from behind a tangle of ferns and creepers. Today the jungle has been pushed back, and the temple has been extensively restored. In the process, much of the romance has been lost, but so too have the popular misconceptions of Pierre Loti and the earlier explorers who first brought the marvels of Angkor to the notice of the western world. We know now that the Bayon was one of the last temples to be built at Angkor, not the first; that it was built at the end of the twelfth century by Jayavarman VII, the last great God-King of the Khmers; that the giant heads are in his likeness; and that the temple was conceived as his personal 'god-mountain', symbol of his divine power, and later his mausoleum. We know that Jayavarman was a Buddhist, that he built more than a hundred hospitals, temples and charitable institutions, and a vast network of roads spanning an empire which stretched from the coast of present-day Vietnam in the east, through Thailand, and up to the border of Pagan in Burma in the west.

Following the reign of Jayavarman VII, the fortunes of the Khmers steadily declined. The burden of building and maintaining a great profusion of temples had left the people exhausted, and in 1431 Angkor was sacked by the Thais and subsequently

The temple of Angkor Wat

abandoned as the Khmer capital. The temples quickly became engulfed by thick jungle and were forgotten until their rediscovery by the French naturalist Henri Mouhot 400 years later.

The Khmer race traces its ancestry to two sources: the 'Lunar Dynasty' of Funan, which arose from the union of an Indian of noble birth with the daughter of a serpent-king; and the 'Solar Dynasty' of Chenla, formed from the union of Kambu, an ascetic, with a celestial nymph named Mera. From Kambuja, 'Sons of Kambu', came the name Cambodia. During the first century AD the Kingdom of Funan, the earliest Hindu state of South-east Asia, was established on the banks of the Mekong river by tribal peoples from southern China, who borrowed Indian techniques of irrigation to drain their land of swamp waters and prepare it for cultivation. By the fifth century, Funan had expanded to the dimensions of an empire, embracing most of present-day Cambodia, Cochin-China, and parts of the Malay Peninsula. At that time the state of Chenla, centred on what is now southern Laos, was a tributary kingdom to Funan, but was rapidly growing in power. In 540 a prince of Funan married a princess of Chenla, uniting the Lunar and Solar dynasties, but in doing so he turned against his own people and seized power for Chenla.

The 'pre-Angkor' period which followed saw a shift in power in the area towards the south, where the island kingdoms of Java and Sumatra were rapidly gaining strength. Towards the end of the eighth century, Chenla became a vassal of Java's Sailendra dynasty. During this time successive capitals were established more and more to the north and away from the sea. Trade with India began to dwindle, and the people turned to the cultivation of rice as their main industry. They began to construct their buildings with brick, decorate them with elegant reliefs, and fill them with statues carved in sandstone, revealing already the serene mastery of material and form that was to achieve its finest expression at Angkor.

The distinction of being the first King of Angkor rests with Jayavarman II, a young Khmer prince who had lived in Java at the court of the Sailendras, builders of the great Borobudur temple. The chronicles suggest that he was quick to proclaim his country's independence of Java, pronouncing himself 'King of the Mountain' and demanding a solemn religious rite to transform him into an incarnation of the great god Shiva. On a hill near Angkor he placed a 'lingam', a large stone phallus, symbol of the creative energy of Shiva, and from that time onwards the container of his 'royal essence' or 'inner self'. With this ceremony he became the first of the God-Kings, the Devaraja, of Angkor, invested with a power which was absolute and with the status of god and king combined.

In the three centuries which followed, successive God-Kings strove to outdo their predecessors by building ever finer and more spectacular temples. So great was their achievement that there is today nowhere in the world which can compare with Angkor for the number, size and perfection of its monuments. Two factors made this possible: the concept of the Devaraja, who could command organised labour on a vast scale; and a system of agricultural hydraulics which ensured that the soil would yield its utmost in a guaranteed succession of rich harvests, and so provide the basis for a thriving economy. Professor Bernard Groslier, who has made a thorough study of Angkor's vast system of reservoirs and irrigation channels, regards the labour bestowed on their construction as 'far more impressive than the building of temples, which were merely chapels crowning a Cyclopean undertaking'.

It was at the end of the eleventh century that Khmer civilisation reached its peak and, with the building of Angkor Wat, its finest expression in art. Angkor Wat is the largest religious building in the world, a gigantic temple-mountain built to the glory of god Vishnu and to serve as mausoleum for his incarnation, the God-King Suryavarman II. As Professor Groslier noted:

'There can be no doubt that it was conceived by one man, by the genius of a great artist. It is a masterpiece without a successor. The disposition of masses is so subtle that this temple constructed of superimposed planes leaps upwards like a pyramid.

'Every stone is decorated with loving care, sometimes indeed to excess, for there is a certain frigidity in these light draperies floating on the surface of the stone. Yet some of the panels are perfect in their grace, for example the "apsaras", the dancing nymphs intertwined in twos and threes along the whole length of the walls. Nude to the waist, they wear skirts of gorgeous material with flying panels spread flat on either side according to the conventional perspective. Nothing can detract from the exquisite grace of their pose, the rhythm of their gestures, the fantastic charm of their plaited tresses and jewelled diadems. They are dream creatures, for whose sake one might almost dare death to enter the paradise in which they disport themselves.'

The God-King was able to enjoy such a paradise even before his death, for he had a retinue of divine nymphs already at his disposal. It was the custom that the loveliest of young girls should be offered by their parents to serve the king as palace dancers and concubines. King Jayavarman VII possessed hundreds of these desirable young maidens, some of whom he offered to his generals in return for heroic deeds on the battlefield. (The reward for a hero killed in battle was the apsaras, the true divine nymph, who awaited him in paradise.)

The beautiful and intricate bas-reliefs which encircle Angkor Wat and the Bayon offer tantalising glimpses of everyday life at Angkor during the twelfth and thirteenth centuries, but it is from the eyewitness report of a Chinese envoy, Chou Ta-kuan, that we may capture the most vivid impression of the city at the height of its greatness:

'When the king rides forth, soldiers march at the head of the procession, followed by the standards, banners and musicians. Next comes a column of three to five hundred palace-maidens, clad in robes of floral pattern, with flowers in their hair and bearing candles, lit even in broad daylight. These are followed by another troop of maidens carrying the royal plate of gold and silver and a whole series of ornaments and insignia. Next come Amazons armed with spears and shields forming the private palace guard – and goats and horse-drawn carriages, all decorated with gold. Then, preceded by innumerable red parasols, visible from afar, come the ministers and the princes, all mounted on elephants, followed by the wives and concubines of the King, some in palanquins and carriages, or mounted on horseback and elephants, their gold-spangled parasols assuredly numbering more than a hundred. Finally the sovereign. He stands erect on an elephant whose tusks are sheathed in gold, and holds the precious sword of state in his hand. He is escorted by more than twenty white parasols, spangled with gold. Numerous elephants mill around him and yet another troop of soldiers provides him protection. . . . From this you may perceive that these people know full well what it is to be a king.'

The photographs of Angkor which follow were taken on 1 January 1979, a few days before the control of Cambodia passed from the Khmer Rouge to the 'liberating' Vietnamese forces.

Between June 1970 and the end of 1978 Angkor had been inaccessible to visitors from the West, and there was concern that the temples might have been damaged during the war and later reclaimed by the jungle. As the pictures show, this has not been the case, and apart from some shell damage, the temples appear to have survived their ordeal.

Would this were true of the Cambodian people. Since 1975 when the Khmer Rouge came to power, a third of the nation's population, and virtually the entire class of artists and educated people, have been systematically eliminated.

ABOVE Angkor Wat: the western approach to the world's largest religious building. This gigantic temple-mountain was built towards the end of the eleventh century to the glory of god Vishnu, and to serve as mausoleum for his incarnation, the God-King Suryavarman II. The temple is a masterpiece without equal, the pinnacle of achievement of the Khmer civilisation

OPPOSITE ABOVE Long corridors encircle Angkor Wat, their walls carved in a profusion of shallow reliefs. Six feet high, over a mile in length, and superbly executed, these rows of carvings rank among the greatest pieces of world sculpture

OPPOSITE BELOW The south wall of the western gallery bears a relief of scenes from the Ramayana. This section, approximately four feet in height, shows the demon-king in his chariot as the battle rages around him

The walls and niches of Angkor Wat are adorned with 2000 reliefs of 'apsarases', the divine nymphs, celestial dancing girls, who waited in paradise to reward men killed heroically in battle. The god-king himself possessed such a retinue – the girls who were his court dancers and, at the same time, his concubines

The mysterious giant heads of the Bayon smile enigmatically towards the surrounding jungle. There have been many theories concerning their identity but it is now generally accepted that they represent the Bodhisattva, Lokesvara, carved in the likeness of the reigning God-King, Suryavarman II, gazing with beneficence towards the four corners of the realm

Three-headed Divinity from one of the gates to the city of Angkor Thom, dating from the end of the 12th century

'Prajnaparamita', a Buddhist divinity, the personification of wisdom, from Preah Khan at Angkor, now in the Musée Guimet, Paris. Almost life-size, it is thought to portray Jayarajadevi, the first wife of King Jayavarman VII

A sandstone statue believed to be in the likeness of Jayavarman VII, the last great God-King of the Khmers. It was found at the Khmer temple of Phimai in Thailand, and now stands in the National Museum in Bangkok

ABOVE One of a row of demons lining the approach to the city of Angkor Thom

RIGHT The south gate to the city of Angkor Thom, surmounted like the Bayon by giant heads of Lokesvara in the likeness of the king, Jayavarman VII. The gate is one of five which penetrate eight miles of stone ramparts

THAILAND
'Country of a Million Buddhas'

In Thailand may be found, at one and the same time, the most up-to-date forms of cultural life in South-east Asia and the most ancient. Whilst young painters in Bangkok struggle to master the latest styles imported from the West, archaeologists in the northern village of Ban Chiang are unearthing pottery and bronze which may prove to be as much as 7000 years old – a discovery which totally shatters existing beliefs concerning the prehistory of South-east Asia. In the Royal Palace, cradle of the traditional arts of court dancing, the reigning monarch writes music for jazz orchestra. At Bangkok's International Airport, a group of highly venerated monks climb into a newly delivered jet-liner to perform a ceremony of blessing and mark it with magical symbols which will protect it from harm.

It is a land of intriguing contrasts. In Bangkok a miniature temple like an oriental doll's house stands on a plinth in front of one of the most strikingly modern buildings in the city. The large building is a hotel, the Siam Intercontinental, a fine example of contemporary Western architecture adapted to an Eastern setting; the small one is a spirit-house, a home for spirits of the land displaced when the hotel was built, and a reminder that the world's oldest religion is still a force in even the most highly developed corners of South-east Asia.

In Thailand the spirits are called 'phi', and they have great potential for evil if they are not properly treated. When another of Bangkok's hotels, the Erawan, was being built, there was a strange and unexplained series of accidents which began to delay the work seriously. A priest was consulted, a sizeable spirit shrine was built on the street corner close to the hotel site, and the troubles ceased. This was so vivid a demonstration of phi power that the Erawan shrine quickly became the most celebrated in the country, and it is daily surrounded by a crowd of people making offerings of candles and garlands of flowers, whilst among them a small group of dancing girls in the glittering costumes of the court perform to the accompaniment of drums and wooden xylophones. To ensure that the spirits will remain friendly, there is no better way than to arrange a dance in their honour. So sacred is the Erawan shrine that a taxi driver is likely to remove both hands from the wheel as he speeds past, in order to make the traditional gesture of prayer, the 'wai', towards the enshrined spirit.

More than ninety per cent of Thais are devoutly

Novice monks in the temple of Doi Sutep, Chiang Mai

Buddhist, and yet the gaily decorative spirit-houses are found beside buildings of all kinds – banks, massage parlours, filling stations, museums, hospitals, the opulent home of one of Bangkok's many business tycoons, or a poor wooden shack beside a canal. Since nobody can prove that spirits do not exist, the Thais prefer to play safe and hedge their bets, and the ceremonies required for a new house consequently take on a religious character which is bewildering to the outsider. First there is a Buddhist ceremony of blessing for the house itself, conducted by monks from a nearby monastery. This is followed by a quite separate ceremony to install the new spirit-house, conducted by a Brahmin priest from a Hindu temple, despite the fact that the spirit who will live in it has more to do with animism and ancestor-worship than with Hinduism. All this is a little easier to understand if one remembers that Buddhism grew out of the Hindu religion, which is itself a highly sophisticated form of the early animism of India, and the common ground allows the three religions to coexist in Thailand, as they do in Burma and far-off Bali.

In ancient times it was the custom to bury a human body beneath the pole which would support a new spirit-house, but nowadays a table of offerings – fish, salad, rice whisky, holy water, incense, and a pig's head – is deemed sufficient. The Brahmin determines an auspicious placing for the spirit-house, somewhere in the garden and as far from the kitchen as possible. He decides also the most auspicious time for the house to be placed in position and for the spirit to take up residence. The house is then filled with a miniature retinue of slaves, horses, cattle and elephants, together with a replica of the residing spirit which should hold a double-edged sword in its right hand. After prayers, accompanied by the blowing of conch shells, the ceremony is at an end, but fresh offerings must be presented to the spirit each evening. For those who may require convincing of the reality of the spirit world, it is a remarkable fact that not one of these delightful residences has ever been taken over by birds.

More than any other country in the world, Thailand is pre-eminent as the land of Buddha images. Produced over a period of 1300 years and ranging in size from tiny miniatures to colossal statues, they are now so numerous that they far outnumber the human population. The majority of Thais wear a tiny amulet, a miniature figure of the Buddha, suspended from a metal chain around the neck, in the belief that it will make them immune from harm. A market area of Bangkok offers these magic charms in a wild profusion of materials, colours, shapes and sizes, together with larger Buddha statues, mass-produced and intended for the domestic family altar. Whatever the image, it is worthless in itself, possessing no power until it has been taken to a monastery for a ceremony which will imbue it with spiritual potency.

The largest and finest images are to be found in the temples, where they are worshipped daily by the devout who come with offerings of flowers and incense and fine wafers of gold leaf to stick on the statues. In doing this they are 'making merit', ensuring an improved status in the next life. To aid the maintenance of a monastery, to make gifts to the needy, to give alms to monks, or even temporarily to enter the monkhood – all such things are considered acts of merit, and as much merit may be gained through a small gift from a poor man as through a great donation from a rich one. It is the intent to make merit that has produced the staggering quantities of Buddha images to be found in Thailand today, ranging in artistic excellence from crude clay tablets, intended for burial inside a monument, to the imposing, larger-than-life images in bronze and gold which occupy the place of honour in the ordination halls of the temples.

Certain of these images are reputed to possess great magical power and to be able to perform miracles, and in general they are worshipped as living beings rather than inanimate objects. The famous Emerald Buddha in Bangkok is given a small wardrobe of clothes to wear – a princely costume for the hot season, a monastic robe for the rainy season, and a mantle of gold mesh for the cool season. The equally celebrated and extremely beautiful 'Jinaraja', 'Victorious King', at Phitsanulok in central Thailand is accredited with having wept tears of blood when the old city of Sukhothai was conquered by the rival kingdom of Ayuthaya. In his book *What is a Buddha Image?* A. B. Griswold describes another curious incident, this time concerning a colossal reclining Buddha, apparently possessed of the power of speech:

> 'One afternoon, in the presence of the Lord Abbot and a large group of monks and novices, deep muffled sounds were heard to issue from its bosom. "Are you not well, Sir?" the Abbot asked politely. The image replied: "Thank you, I am quite well: and you?" "Sir, I am well." "But trouble is on its way," said the image: "within two months there will be a bad outbreak of cholera." Upon being asked what countermeasures could be taken, the image provided a recipe to be compounded from certain herbs; and when the cholera came, exactly as predicted, the medicine proved to be an effective cure.'

Buddha images do not always behave so usefully:

> 'Certain of the most famous ones were very unpredictable, and often downright cranky, acting in a way the Buddha himself would have condemned in the strongest terms. Like powerful spirits, they gave material rewards when flattered and made much of, but in moments of annoyance inflicted disease, set buildings on fire, and caused earthquakes. The Emerald Buddha and the Pra Bang Buddha are said to have detested each other, and caused all sorts of trouble, including a brief revolution, so they had to be separated.'

Buddha images not only behave as powerful spirits; that, in effect, is what they are. Certainly, by their appearance, they offer a reminder of the Buddha himself, of his life and his teaching, but the Buddha is not a god. When he entered Nirvana he ceased to exist, and he is therefore unable to listen to the prayers of his devoted followers. Under the official cloak of Buddhism, the devout Thai who prostrates himself before an image of Buddha is in fact seeking the good will of the spirits.

The Thais are a fiercely independent people, and justly proud that theirs is the only country in South-east Asia never to have been a European colony. But this had not always been the land of the Thais: many peoples were here before them, and the astonishing finds at Ban Chiang suggest that a mysterious civilisation of unknown origin flourished in this part of Asia as early as 5000 BC. These are the realms of prehistory, but in historic times the most powerful cultural influence has been that of India. Between the sixth and twelfth centuries AD, the so-called 'Dvaravati' period, the Buddhist religion became firmly established in those parts of the country ruled by the 'Mon' people, who may themselves have been of Indian origin, and a small number of stone sculptures of the Buddha survive from that time.

The next peoples to arrive were the Khmers, whose spectacular temples still stand in Lopburi and Phimai. Connected to Angkor by elevated military roads, with rest-houses at ten-mile intervals, these were the outposts of a mighty empire. By the middle of the twelfth century the ruler of Angkor, God-King Suryavarman II, had become one of the most powerful men in Asia, second only to the Emperor of China.

While the Khmer were consolidating their hold on the southern Mon region, the Thais were gaining strength in the north of the country. Their homeland was Yunan, a province of China, but for many years they had been steadily moving south, away from their oppressive Chinese overlords, establishing small independent kingdoms as they went. They brought with them a belief in spirits of nature and of ancestors similar to the early 'Nat' worship in Burma, and appear at first to have had little knowledge of Buddhism. The most powerful of the early Thai kingdoms were those of Chiang Mai, in the mountainous north, and Sukhothai, on the central plains.

Here were laid the foundations of the nation which was later to become Thailand. The first great king of the Thais was Ramkamhaeng, and under his benevolent rule in the thirteenth century Sukhothai became an important centre of art and learning. The city is now a jumble of beautiful and evocative ruins, but a stone inscription describes the days of its glory:

> 'This Sukhothai is good. In the water there are fish, in the fields there is rice. The king does not levy a rate on his people. . . . Who wants to trade in elephants, trades. Who wants to trade in horses, trades. Who wants to trade in gold and silver, trades. The faces of the people shine bright.'

At the height of its power, Sukhothai governed an empire which extended as far south as the Malay peninsula, but following the death of Ramkamhaeng the city was forced to relinquish its pride of place to Ayuthaya, a rapidly growing kingdom in the south-east, which maintained control of the country for the next 400 years. When, in the early seventeenth century, the English first set foot in the capital, they were greatly impressed:

> 'It was a surprising place upon which to come suddenly – as great a city as London – larger than Paris with poor houses, magnificent pagodas, an admirable river, a huge population, and with countless boats. Walls were of stone, main streets broad and straight on a regular plan with canals running down one side, and the King's palace was like a town apart, great and magnificent, many of its buildings and towers being entirely gilded.'

Ayuthaya was built on an island formed by the confluence of three rivers, and it was clearly a place of the greatest splendour. In his book *Thailand* Hans Johannes Hoeffer writes:

> 'It had nearly 400 temples, in which Thai art and architecture reached their full flowering, glittering with gold and multi-coloured tiles and mosaics; down its 55 kilometres of waterways moved the stately royal barges, carved in the shapes of fabulous animals, along with thousands of humbler craft; 47 kilometres of paved roads accommodated ornate palanquins carrying noblemen and massive war elephants with their jewelled harnesses; and 19-cannon fortresses made it seem – erroneously as it turned out – as impregnable as it was impressive.'

In 1767 Ayuthaya fell to an invading Burmese army, which proceeded to loot the city in a mindless rampage of destruction. By the time they had finished, nothing remained beyond a mass of smoking ruins. Gone were the magnificent palaces and temples, and the treasures of painting and lacquer-work they had contained. Valuable manuscripts bearing the written history of the Thai people were almost completely destroyed, and the finest artists – painters, dancers and musicians – had been carried off to serve at the court of the Burmese king. It was an act of vandalism without parallel, and one of which the Thais are ever-mindful, but within a few years they had succeeded in driving out the Burmese and establishing a new capital at Thonburi, which now faces Bangkok across the broad expanse of the Chao Phya river. The man responsible for this great victory was a soldier named Taksin and he promptly set himself up as king. His reign was short-lived: after ten years he went insane and was executed in the manner prescribed for royalty – being placed in a velvet sack and beaten to death with a sandalwood club.

The successor to Taksin was King Rama I, founder of the Chakri dynasty which still occupies the Thai throne. (The present ruler, King Bhumiphol, is Rama IX.) Rama I established his new capital at Bangkok, 'City of Angels', in 1782, and there he set about recreating the glories of Ayuthaya, still fresh in memory. Rama I was a man of learning and a patron of the arts. He composed the first modern version of the Ramayana in Siamese, and his reign marked the beginning of a period in which the noble arts of courtly dance, the Khon and the Lakhon, were raised to great heights of artistic expression.

Khon is based on the Thai version of the Ramayana, the 'Ramakien' ('The Fame of Rama'), and it survives as the oldest form of theatre in Thailand. Like the ancient temple dances of India from which it developed, it uses a language of gesture to interpret the action of the story, relying upon singers among the accompanying instruments to provide the dialogue. Khon, literally 'Mask', makes much use of a large variety of masks which express the personalities of the characters – monkeys, demons, holy men – and which are themselves revered as sacred objects. Nowadays performers acting the parts of heroes and celestial beings no longer use masks, but wear instead high crowns or painted head-dresses.

Lakhon Nai is a pure dance traditionally performed within the palace by the king's special harem, and deriving from the court dances of Cambodia. A little over 200 years ago, Siam conquered that neighbouring kingdom and brought back to the Thai capital a troupe of Cambodian palace dancers. Ironically they were probably reimporting a commodity which had originated in the south of Thailand nearly 1000 years before and had been taken to Angkor by the early Khmer king, Suryavarman I. The dancers portrayed in the bas-reliefs of Angkor Wat are prototypes of the Thai dancers of today. To add a final chapter to this artistic to-ing and fro-ing, the palace dancers now to be found in Cambodia are themselves a result of re-importation from Thailand, following a further stage of refinement in the courts of the Chakri dynasty.

In 1932, the absolute monarchy which had ruled Thailand since the establishment of the first Thai Kingdom of Sukhothai 700 years earlier came to an end, and King Rama VII agreed to serve under a constitutional government. The court was no longer able to support its large and costly troupe of dancers, and it was left to the universities and the government-sponsored School of Dramatic Arts to ensure that the ancient traditions of dance-theatre would not disappear. Today the school preserves the Khon and Lakhon, together with numerous folk-dances from all parts of the country. Beside the school of dance is a sister school, dedicated to preserving the ancient music of Thailand, and both offer their students a general education from the ages of eight to eighteen in addition to their tuition in music and dance. It is typical of this land of contrasts that, in a city throbbing to the sound of disco music, there are more potential students for the excruciatingly demanding disciplines of classical dance than the schools can accommodate.

ABOVE AND OPPOSITE Dawn at Sukhothai, central Thailand

OVERLEAF Wat Mahathat, Sukhothai

In the days of its glory, Sukhothai was the centre of a giant empire stretching from the north of Thailand to the Malay peninsula. Its founding, in the early 13th century, marks the beginning of the Thai nation as we know it today. It grew to become a famous centre of art and learning; the first Thai alphabet was devised here, and sculpture reached a peak of perfection which was never to be surpassed in later years. The temples which filled the city had high, multi-tiered roofs – they were the forerunners of the ornate buildings now characteristic of Thai architecture. The greatest king of Sukhothai was Ramkamhaeng, a benevolent monarch who, it is said, placed a bell outside his palace gate, and anyone with a grievance had only to ring it to gain a royal audience

Early each morning in Chiang Mai the monks receive alms from the people of the city, especially the women, who earn merit by their giving.

It is the custom that all young men should enter a monastery as an essential part of their education even if it is for no longer than a month. There, bereft of material possessions, they practise meditation and study the teachings of Buddha

ABOVE Walking Buddha, Wat Benchamabopit, Bangkok. The sculptors of Sukhothai did not aim at a lifelike representation of the Buddha, but tried instead to emphasise the other-worldly respects of the 'Exalted One, whose steps levelled the ground and brought forth lotus blossoms'. This image is one of the finest pieces of Thai art in existence

OPPOSITE A folk dance of the Phu Thai tribe of north-east Thailand

OPPOSITE The 'Sern Kayang', or Bamboo Basket dance, of the Kalasin people of north-east Thailand

The classical dances of Thailand, nurtured for centuries within the royal palaces, are now kept alive by universities and schools of music and dancing. Children begin their training at 7 or 8, when their limbs are still supple enough to be manipulated into the sharply angular gestures required of a classical dancer. By the time they leave the school 10 years later they will have received a general education, in addition to a knowledge of every classical and folk dance in the repertoire

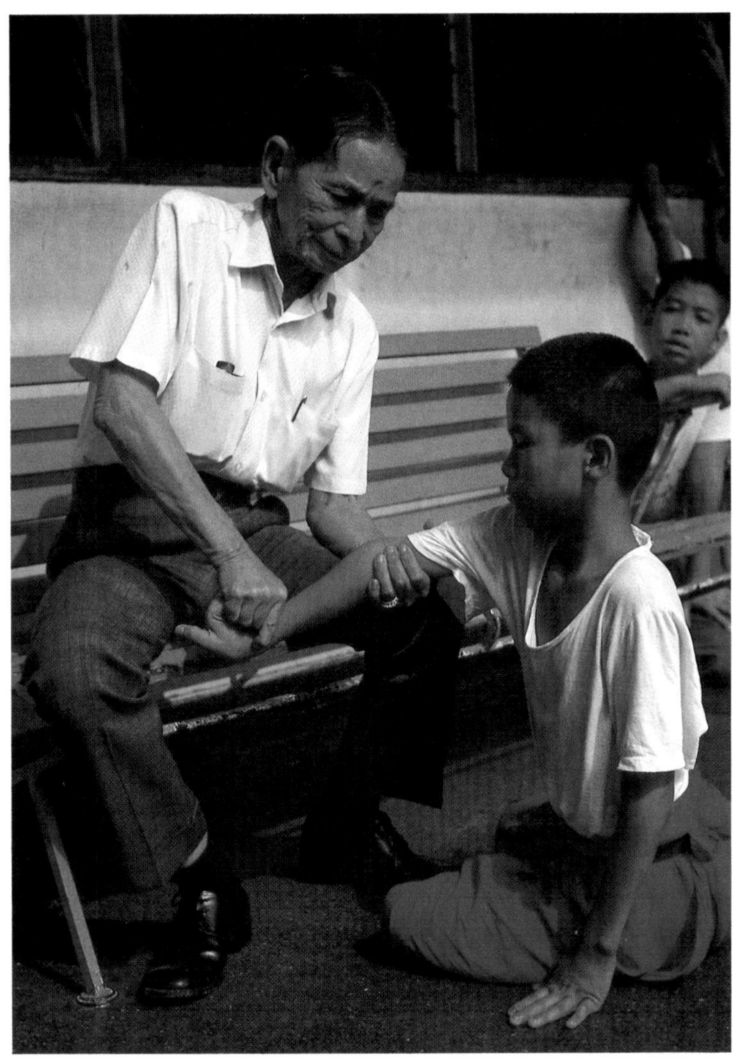

ABOVE The 'Khon' is the oldest form of theatre still existing in Thailand. Like India's Kathakali, it is based on the Ramayana epic, here called 'Ramakien', and uses hand gestures – 'mudras' – to add meaning to the words of the accompanying song. Because the Ramayana is Hindu and they are Buddhist, the Thais regard the story simply as a fairy tale, a part of their non-religious tradition

OPPOSITE A girl from Bangkok's School of Dancing takes the role of heroine in a student play about the wars between Thailand and Burma which, in 1767, resulted in the wanton destruction of Ayuthaya

The agile monkey army of the Ramakien story. Very soon after joining the school, a young student is given the role which suits him best – king, demon, hero, monkey – and he will play that part throughout his dancing life

A bronze image of the Bodhisattva 'Avalokiteshvara', from Chaiya, south Thailand, a product of the 8th-century Srivijaya school. Height 63 cm

In the artistically inventive 'Mahayana' Buddhism there are innumerable Bodhisattvas – spiritual beings who are one step short of Buddhahood. Having reached enlightenment they refuse to abandon other beings to their suffering – with compassion, they stay in the world to help

An image of the Buddha in stone, Dvaravati school (7th–9th century), a rare masterpiece of the Mon people. Its style is based on that of India under the Gupta dynasty – a broad face with flat nose and thick lips, elongated eyes, and eyebrows joined in a sharp ridge to form an arc with a triple curve

In Bangkok a person who buys a new car will often take it to the monastery to be blessed – a prudent measure in a city with an accident rate of frightening proportions

When a house is built, a home must be provided for the spirit of the land who has been displaced by the building. In ancient times it was the custom to bury a human body beneath the pole which would support a new spirit-house, but nowadays a table of offerings is considered sufficient. The spirit who will take up residence is represented by a small golden image carrying a double-edged sword

OPPOSITE 'Jinaraja', the 'Victorious King', is the highly venerated Buddha image of Phitsanulok in central Thailand, said to have wept tears of blood when the old city of Sukhothai was conquered by the rival kingdom of Ayuthaya

The reclining Buddha of Nakhon Pathom, west of Bangkok. The largest and finest images are to be found in the temples, where they are worshipped daily by the devout, who make offerings of flowers and incense and fine wafers of gold leaf to stick on the statues. In doing so the people are making merit, ensuring themselves of an improved status in the next life

The 'klongs', canals, of Bangkok are often no more than a stone's throw from the congested streets and high-rise buildings of the city centre, but they seem a world apart. Here, and in the many palace and monastery gardens scattered throughout the city, one can still discover a life of beauty and tranquillity

ความรักคือเทพเจ้า
ความใคร่คือปีศาจ
Love is divine
Lust is devil.
ความรักที่เริ่มต้น-
ด้วยมิตรภาพ
ประกันตัวมันเอง
Love that begins
with friendship is
its own guarantee

In the New Year festival of 'Songkran', a float bearing the Songkran Queen and her attendants is taken through Chiang Mai in a seemingly endless procession of revellers. Everywhere they are met by a deluge of water, from children with water pistols, girls with plastic buckets, and men with fire hoses. The water is a symbol of abundance – in creating their artificial monsoon, the people are asking the gods to send rain in the months ahead, and so provide them with a rich harvest

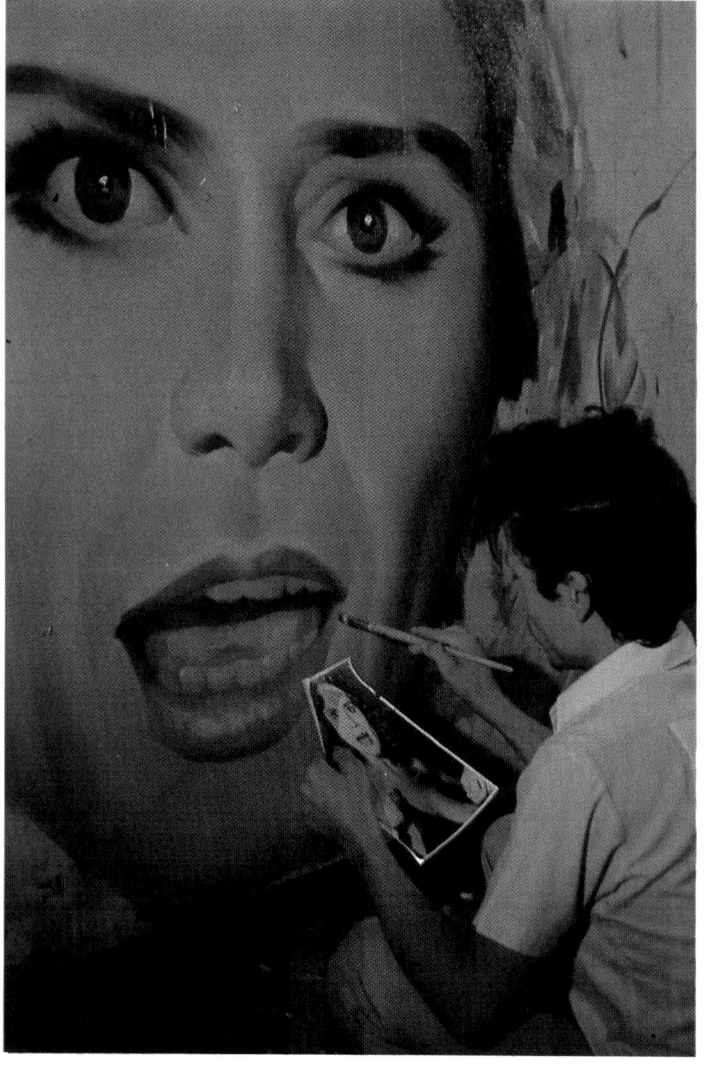

The larger-than-life cinema posters of Bangkok are all hand-painted. The artists work in teams with black and white photographs, each man being responsible for one section of the poster under the overall supervision of a designer. Typically, a team of 11 men will complete a poster in 3 days.

The posters are used many times over. When screenings in the capital come to an end, poster and film travel the country together

OVERLEAF Lakon Nai is a dance traditionally performed within the palace by girls of the king's harem. It derives from the court dances of Cambodia, which themselves had developed from the earlier dances of Thailand.

M. R. Kukrit Pramoj is a member of the Thai royal family and a past prime minister of Thailand. The masks he holds belong to the 10-headed demon Tosakanth (Ravana). It has 9 faces – the face of the wearer being the 10th

OVERLEAF Within the walls of the Grand Palace a mythical creature, the 'Kinaree', half-bird, half-woman, guards the Royal Pantheon

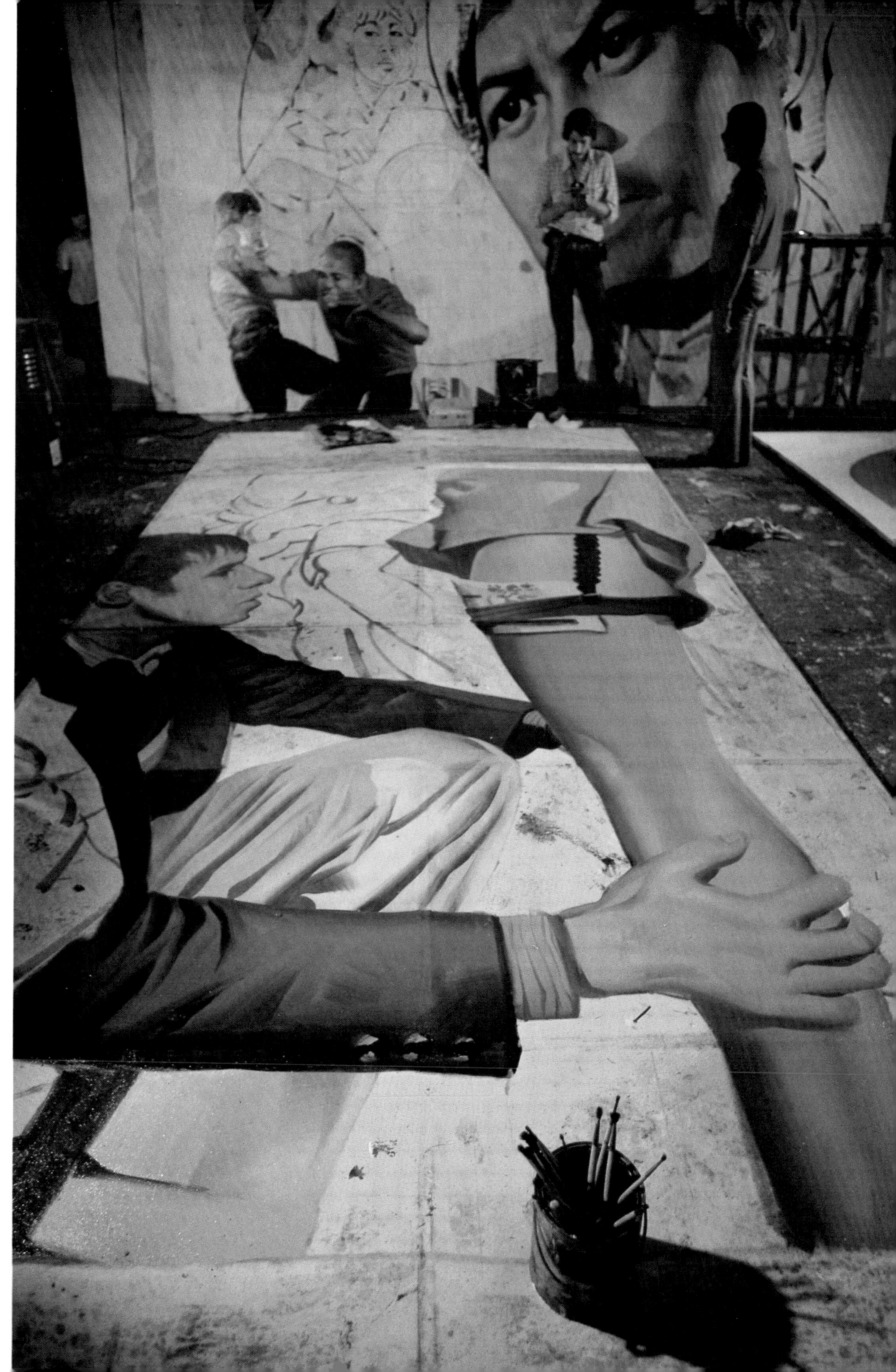

With its cluster of spires glinting in the sunlight, Bangkok's Grand Palace epitomises the popular conception of Siamese regal splendour. It was built in 1782 by King Rama I, a replica of the palace in Ayuthaya destroyed by the Burmese 15 years earlier, but later kings added buildings and embellishments of their own, and the palace today reflects the tastes of 9 generations

ABOVE A scene from the life of Buddha, portrayed in gold and black lacquer, one of the few examples of the art of Ayuthaya to escape the Burmese invasion of 1767. Dating from the 17th century, it forms part of the decoration of a monastery building, now the property of Princess Chumbhot of Nagara Svarga

OPPOSITE ABOVE In Wat Pra Singh, the most eminent monastery of Chiang Mai, mural paintings of the early 19th century illustrate the 'Jatakas' – moral tales of the Buddha's previous existences, before the life when he attained supreme enlightenment

OPPOSITE BELOW The monks of Chiang Mai still decorate the walls of their monasteries, but the style of painting has changed greatly. In Wat U Mong, a teaching monastery which uses illustrations derived from every major religion of the world, this allegorical work is one monk's vision of the human condition

ABOVE The 16th-century Wat Prathat, built on a hilltop near Chiang Mai. The central tower, or 'chedi', is 24 metres high and covered with engraved gold tiles

OPPOSITE A golden image of the Buddha dressed as a Thai king and using the gesture of the hands which means 'dispelling fear'. 18th–19th century, Bangkok period

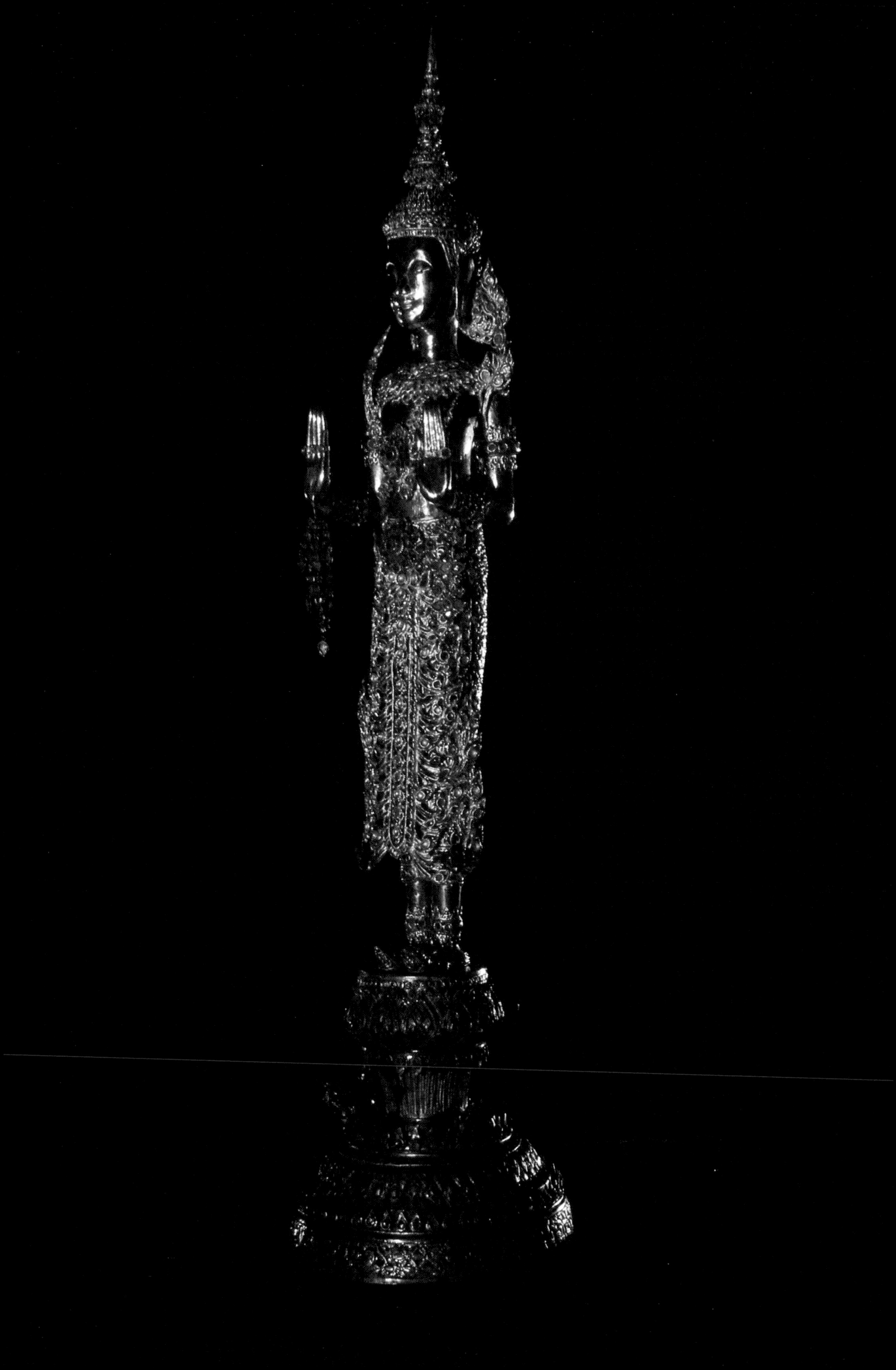

BURMA
'Buddha and the Lords of the Earth'

Just as the Hinduism of Bali is underlaid by animism and magic, so the Buddhism of Burma goes hand in hand with the worship of the Nats – literally 'Lords' – spirits of trees, rivers, stones, the ghosts of ancestors, and Burmese versions of the Hindu gods. Images of the Nats have been carved in wood, painted on temple walls, and cast in bronze, silver and gold, and their worship has given a special character to Burmese art.

Since the coup of 1962 which placed General Ne Win in power, Burma has chosen to follow its own 'Road to Socialism' in virtual isolation from the rest of the world, and in the main closed to visitors. Consequently, few people in the West today can be aware of its wealth of temples, or the vitality of its theatre, dance and music – such as the virtuoso brilliance of the solo music improvised on a circle of twenty-one tuned drums. Its landscape is as beautiful and its people as friendly and hospitable as any in Asia, and there is the added fascination of a country where time, it seems, has stood still. In the cities the faded colonial façades and World War 2 jeeps evoke the late forties, while in the countryside laden bullock carts lumber through landscapes dotted with pagodas and unchanged through centuries.

The capital is Rangoon, situated in the south of the country on the flat, low-lying delta of the great Irrawaddy river. It is a city of decaying splendour, its finest buildings, put up a century ago for the British Raj, now taken over by shopkeepers or turned into tenements. Old taxis rattle through the streets, their Indian drivers travelling in pairs, ready for the inevitable breakdown. On the swiftly flowing waters of the Irrawaddy, ancient steam trading vessels appear to be bursting their boilers in a desperate attempt to make headway upstream. By the roadside, old ladies with deeply wrinkled faces sell fat cheroots, whilst palmists cater to the Burmese fascination with astrology and water-sellers strain their life-giving liquid through a muslin bag. There are nearly three million people living in Rangoon, but there is a gentleness and a calm about the place which seem somehow inappropriate to a capital city, and there could hardly be a greater contrast than that between Rangoon and its neighbour Bangkok. Here there are no bars, no massage parlours, no nightlife, and since most businesses are nationalised, no hectoring advertisements.

Daily life in Burma is characterised by two basic needs: on the one hand, to appease the spirits so that

Landscape near Mandalay

they will not make trouble; and on the other, to accumulate merit through good works, and so ensure a better life in the next incarnation. As in Thailand, the favourite method of gaining merit is to give to the temples, here called pagodas, and to the monasteries. Early every morning long processions of monks in their saffron robes file through the city from door to door, their black offering bowls in one hand, while the other holds up a fan to shelter their shaven heads from the sun. At every door they receive rice – to become a monk is one way to win merit, to give to a monk is another.

In Burma every boy must become a monk and enter a monastery, if only for a week, and the day of his initiation is considered one of the most important in his life. The preparations are elaborate. He must have his face carefully made up, and be dressed as a prince, the greatest possible contrast to the life of abstinence and poverty that he is about to follow. On his arms and shoulders he wears decorations of gilded leather like flames, symbols of power carried by the spirits which lend him also a supernatural presence. For this costly day of celebration – 'Shin Pyu' – many families band together so that all of their sons should receive initiation at the same time, and when make-up and dressing are finished, the boys are carried on the shoulders of their older brothers in a magnificent procession around the platform of the pagoda. After prayers to the Nats and to Buddha, they are taken in a motor cavalcade to the monastery, where their heads will be shaven, their princely costumes changed for plain saffron robes, and with vows of chastity, abstention and obedience, they will begin their life as monks.

Not only young boys are initiated on this day, but older men too, for many choose to return to the monastery at particular times of their lives – after a bereavement, in order to study, or to seek refuge from the turmoil of the outside world. All must have their heads shaved, for the Buddha wished all mankind to be equal, and princes and commoners are indistinguishable when shaven-headed and clad in saffron.

The skyline above Rangoon is dominated by a gigantic inverted cone of gold – the stupa of the great Schwe Dagon pagoda. The Schwe Dagon is the spiritual heart of Burma. Tradition maintains that it was miraculously founded at the very moment that the Buddha received his enlightenment and that beneath its vast, solid mound of brickwork there lie some sacred hairs from his head. Certainly it is the largest and oldest shrine of its kind in the world. For a thousand years the kings of Burma have striven to acquire merit by building the Schwe Dagon still higher and adding yet more layers of gold to the glittering sheath that encases it. Its spire today rises over 300 feet, and at its top it carries an orb studded with more than 4000 diamonds. The very pinnacle of the pagoda is the tip of a 76-carat diamond of the first water.

Around the main platform of the pagoda there are seven sections, each sacred to a particular day of the week. All Burmese know from consulting an astrologer that one of those days is of supernatural importance to them, and it is in the corner dedicated to their particular day that they must worship, by pouring water over the Buddha images – a form of homage demanded in ancient times by the Nats.

The Burmese Nat has never enjoyed great popularity among the rulers of the country. As early as the eleventh century Anawrahta, King of Pagan, tried to eradicate Nat worship, but without success. Forced to realise that the old religion still maintained a powerful hold on the people, he ordered that Buddha himself be enshrined as a Nat. 'Men will not come for the sake of the new faith, let them come for their old gods and gradually they will be won over.' But they were not won over, and Nat worship continues to this day, much to the embarrassment of educated people, the more devout Buddhists, and the Burmese Government.

'As a simple matter of fact it is undeniable that the propitiating of the Nats is a question of daily concern to the lower-class Burman, while the worship at the pagoda is only thought of once a week. For the Nat may prove destructive and hostile at any time, whereas the acquisition of merit at the pagoda is a thing which may be set about in a business-like way, and at proper and convenient seasons.' (Sir George Scott during the time of British colonial rule.)

Until quite recently, a man giving evidence in a Burmese court of law was obliged to swear on the 'Book of the Oath', which made frequent mention of the Nats and the punishment they would mete out if he did not speak the whole truth and nothing but:

'May the Nats who watch and ward the mighty rivers, the lesser streams, the lakes, the torrents, cataracts, and whirlpools; the Nats who preside over the vast forests and the single trees; the Nats of the sun, the moon, the stars and meteors, the clouds, winds, mists, and exhalations; may the naga [serpent] and the galón [griffin], hideous dragons, and cruel birds, all batús [ogres], demons, warlocks, all the evils that come from within the body; may all these spirits and ill things unite to slay me and mine, to the utmost limits of kinship, if I speak not the truth.'

Originally, the Nats were without number, but by the eleventh century they had been canonised into exactly thirty-six, each with his own history and personality, plus the Buddha as an honorary thirty-seventh. One of the most famous is the Mahagiri Nat, originally a blacksmith who was so strong he could pull out an elephant's tusk. After many adventures he was murdered by a jealous king. To placate his angry spirit, a special home was provided for him on Mt Popa, a sharp pinnacle of volcanic rock which rises dramatically from the arid landscape of Upper Burma. At the summit of the mountain is a cluster of temples, and here, once a year, a festival of dancing is held in honour of the Nats. The dancers, who are mediums, are given offerings and, becoming possessed by whichever Nat has chosen them, enter a state of trance. Then, as they dance, they communicate the wishes of the Nat to all present. Apparently female Nats prefer to inspire male dancers, whilst male Nats gravitate to females, a situation which has led to a demand for transvestite dancers.

Near Mt Popa, on the east bank of the Irrawaddy river, lies the ancient capital of Pagan. A thousand years ago, when the power of Burma was at its height, Pagan was one of the greatest religious centres in the whole of South-east Asia. For twenty miles the Irrawaddy was lined with a dense assembly of temples. Once there were over 13,000 of them, and even today it is possible to count the ruins of some 5000. Successive rulers tried to outdo their predecessors by building bigger and better temples, and by doing so hoped to gain much merit in the next life. It was the royal conceit that a king who had built a sufficiently fine pagoda would himself achieve Buddhahood at his death:

'Who favours and upholds like me the gift of faith which I thus offer with all my heart, may such, like me, be favoured above others with the wheel of treasure; may he be endowed like King Mandhata with glory, majesty, and power, may he receive the boon of Buddhahood, of sainthood. . . . But whoever even spoils so much as an oil lamp out of the glebe I have offered, may he be oppressed with the eight dangers, the ten punishments, the thirty-two results of Karma, the eight calamities, the ninety-six diseases. May he be suddenly overtaken with great affliction which a thousand doctors may not avail to cure . . . !'

This frightening imprecation held no terrors for Kublai Khan. In 1287 his armies sacked the city, and the days of Pagan's glory were at an end. But many of the pagodas were spared, and the finest of them all, the Ananda, has been in constant use since its consecration at the end of the eleventh century.

The Ananda pagoda is a massive yet graceful structure, dazzlingly white and with a spire of gold. Its base is pierced by concentric grids of corridors, lined with golden plaques illustrating the life of the

Buddha. On each side of a gigantic solid cone stand golden figures of the Buddha, thirty feet high.

On 8 July 1975, disaster struck Pagan in the form of a powerful earthquake. Rents appeared in walls; Buddha images split in two; tall spires rocked and crashed to the ground. More than 1000 temples were severely damaged. It will take many years to repair the results of those few minutes of violence, but already a great deal has been achieved. The shattered dome of the Ananda pagoda has been given a lining of reinforced concrete and a new bronze umbrella, whilst the Bupaya pagoda, which had crumbled into nothing more than a pile of dust, has been completely rebuilt by the people of the village which surrounds it. The restoration work seems assured of a continuing supply of funds and manpower – to help in the rebuilding of a pagoda is to earn great merit.

The furnishings of the pagodas – the Buddha images, and the gold leaf to stick on them – are made in Mandalay, a great centre for crafts and cultural activities of all kinds. By the roadside carvers sit astride enormous marble Buddhas, chipping away at their glacial features with chisels. In conditions of choking dust and heat, bronze-casters turn out Buddha images by the dozen, using the 'lost wax' technique perfected 2000 years ago.

In the centre of Mandalay are the walls and moat of the Imperial Palace, last occupied by King Thibaw, who was deposed by the British in 1885 on the pretext that he was a barbarous tyrant. Decapitation and disembowelling were not uncommon, and men sentenced to death were forced to place their heads on a tree stump to be stepped on by a royal elephant. Punishments such as these were carried out within the palace grounds amid a maze of wooden buildings superbly decorated with the most intricate carving. Not for the first time, barbarism went hand in hand with a refined taste in matters artistic. Today nothing remains of those wooden buildings apart from a small monastery removed from the palace for use elsewhere. During World War 2, the Japanese occupied the palace and it required a bomb attack to dislodge them. The buildings were burned to the ground.

In April each year, when the weather is oppressively hot and dry, the people celebrate Thingyan, 'the transition from the old year to the new', and they do it by gleefully throwing water at one another. In the past young men dipped flowers into scented water in silver bowls, and sprinkled it on young damsels. Today they use a battery of fire hoses! Roadside stages are put up throughout the city and used for dancing at night and the spraying of water by day. It is one of the world's most astonishing spectacles as the ancient jeeps, crammed with pretty girls in clinging 'longyis', form up in long queues in front of these stages and take their turn to run a gauntlet of hoses, water pistols and buckets of water. Soaked to the skin, they spend the day driving from one watering point to another.

From 6 pm no more water may be thrown, and the people go home and dry off, ready for the celebrations of the evening. By the time they have returned to the streets, the roadside stages have been transformed. Fire hoses have vanished, sumptuous carpets cover the wooden boards, and small orchestras of drums and gongs have been placed in position at the back of each stage. Shortly after dark the entertainment begins. It takes the form of alternate dancing and chanting. The dances are performed by large troupes of young girls, resplendent in ankle-length gowns of pale blue or pink and sparkling with sequins. Their movements are lively and angular, and resemble those of marionettes. The chanting, a uniquely Burmese form of expression, is performed by teams of young men on motorised floats, which drive through the city from one stage to another. At each stage they are entertained by a dance, and then they begin their chant – a form of question and answer with a cheer leader bellowing his questions into a megaphone, and his twenty to thirty companions howling back their reply in unison. In a country where criticism of the government is actively discouraged, this is the one time in the year when the people can air their grievances in public.

'We must seriously think about our problems.'
'We must criticise thoroughly.'
'Why are students taking private tuition?'
'Why is the lottery always won by the boss of the co-operative?'
'Why do private doctors have medicines and the hospitals have none?'

'If you hold it, it is thorny;
'If you eat it, you will go mad;
If you smell it, you will go dizzy;
If you want to buy it, it is expensive;
If you use it, you will die.'

'What is it? The Bedaine fruit?'
'No! It is the dreadful heroin number 4.'

The dances, the chanting and the water-throwing continue for four days, and by the end of the festival everyone feels much better. The rivalries, jealousies, frustrations and resentments, accumulated over twelve months, have been given release, and the Buddha and the spirits have received their due. In a few weeks the monsoon will arrive, with torrential rains to fill the dried-up beds of rivers and lakes and refresh the rice fields. In this habitually tranquil land life returns to normal.

Burma's isolationist policies have been much criticised, but they do have the redeeming achievement of having protected the people from the dehumanising influence of mass tourism and commercial exploitation, and have helped preserve a charm and tranquillity rarely found nowadays in the neighbouring countries

In villages clustered around Mandalay and the ancient capital, Pagan, skilled craftsmen continue to produce Buddha images in bronze and marble and to decorate bamboo lacquer-ware with traditional designs. The techniques they use are many centuries old

A thousand years ago Pagan was one of the greatest religious centres in the whole of South-east Asia. Successive rulers tried to outdo their predecessors by building bigger and better temples, and by doing so hoped to gain great merit – perhaps even to achieve Buddhahood.

For 20 miles along the east bank of the Irrawaddy river and for 5 miles inland, magnificent temples punctuated the landscape. Once there were over 13,000 of them, and even today one can count the ruins of some 5000

A pagoda was built not primarily as a place of worship but as the home of a god. The people of Pagan knew that Mt Meru was the dwelling place of the gods of India, just as their Mt Popa was the home of the Burmese 'Nat' spirits. On adopting the Indian religion they therefore began to build their pagodas in the likeness of Mt Meru, and place within them images, plaques and paintings as constant reminders of the divine presence

ABOVE Near Mandalay, pagodas line the banks of the Irrawaddy river

OPPOSITE From the forests of Upper Burma, teak logs are floated down to Rangoon as rafts

The Irrawaddy, one of the great rivers of Asia, rises on the southern rim of Tibet, flows south for 1000 miles, and empties into the sea between India, to the west, and Thailand, to the east. The chief trade route between Rangoon and the mountainous jungle of Upper Burma, the Irrawaddy is Kipling's 'Road to Mandalay'

ABOVE At Amerapura, near Mandalay, an old wooden bridge a mile long crosses an expanse of arable land which, in the rainy season, disappears beneath the waters of a lake

OPPOSITE At one end of the bridge stands a small pagoda honey-combed with alcoves, each containing a Buddha image

Amerapura was the Burmese capital 150 years ago, and it was from here that the first British residents sent home reports of a city of white pagodas and splendidly carved wooden palaces

At the foot of a guardian lion at the Schwe Dagon pagoda, a young monk silently mouths the Buddhist liturgies as he counts the beads of a rosary

OVERLEAF The Schwe Dagon is the spiritual heart of Burma, the largest and oldest shrine of its kind in the world. Tradition maintains that it was miraculously founded at the very moment that the Buddha received his enlightenment, and that beneath its vast, solid mound of brickwork lie some sacred hairs from his head

In Burma every boy must become a monk, if only for a week, and the day of his initiation is one of the most important in his life. He must have special make-up for his face and be dressed as a prince, the greatest possible contrast to the life of abstinence and poverty which he is to follow. On days declared auspicious by astrologers, the parents of young boys band together, so that their sons may receive initiation at the same time, and large groups of young 'princes' converge on the Schwe Dagon pagoda to pray to images of the Buddha and the Nats, and to pose for family photographs. Among them are small girls, also in courtly dress, who will receive a token initiation by ear-piercing

Leaving the pagoda, the boys are taken to a monastery where they are divested of their regalia and their heads are shaved, as the Buddha had done 2500 years earlier when he abandoned the life of a prince and set out to discover the true nature of human suffering. Finally, the boys are dressed in saffron robes and, with vows of abstention and obedience, they begin their life as monks

For a child of 4, the experience of leaving home and entering a monastery may be frightening and bewildering but later he may come to appreciate the value of a religious retreat

OPPOSITE The walls and moat of the Imperial Palace of Mandalay once enclosed a maze of wooden buildings superbly decorated with finely-detailed carvings, but in World War 2 the Japanese occupied the palace and it required a bomb attack to dislodge them. Today nothing remains of those buildings apart from the gate-houses and a small monastery removed from the palace before the war

The Burmese celebrate the New Year, as do the Thais, by drenching each other in water – but here the dousing is more thorough. It is as if the pent-up frustrations of the past 12 months at last achieve a release in this one glorious deluge

ABOVE On Lake Inle in the hills of Shan State in east Burma, the fishermen have devised a method of leg-rowing which leaves the hands free to handle a net

OPPOSITE To the west, on the banks of the Irrawaddy river, one of the myriad temples of Sagaing reflects the brilliance of the midday sun

OVERLEAF The Irrawaddy at Pagan

The outgoing warmth and gentle humour of the Burmese have endowed their dances with a charm and vitality which make them instantly enjoyable. They say you cannot dance if you are feeling sad, and they make no attempt to portray the deeper emotions of sorrow or anger. Instead, their dances are gay and exuberant, with angularly acrobatic movements like those of the marionettes they sometimes impersonate, performed in short, sudden outbursts of explosive energy

Mt Popa, a sharp pinnacle of rock jutting out of the arid landscape of the upper Irrawaddy valley, is crowned with a cluster of monasteries and pagodas. It is the home of the Mahagiri Nats, a celebrated family of ancestor-spirits, and here the people come to bestow offerings on the Nats and, once a year, to make contact with them through spirit mediums

Originally the Nats were without number, but by the 11th century they had been canonised into a pantheon of 36, each with his own history and personality, plus the Buddha as an honorary 37th.

In the annual Nat festival of Mt Popa, dancers in trance become possessed by the particular spirit which has chosen them as a human vehicle – male dancers are possessed by female spirits, female dancers by male spirits. This dancer, who portrays the 'Mother of Mt Popa', is a man, a medical practitioner from Rangoon

ACKNOWLEDGEMENTS

I would like to thank the National Museum in Bangkok, the Musée Guimet and the Petit Palais in Paris, and the Tropen Museum in Amsterdam, for their permission to photograph pieces in their collections.

The museum shots were taken during filming, and I am all too aware of the debt I owe to the BBC cameramen Philip Bonham-Carter and Nat Crosby, whose sensitive lighting of the sculptures was of infinitely greater importance than the actual taking of the photographs.

M.M.

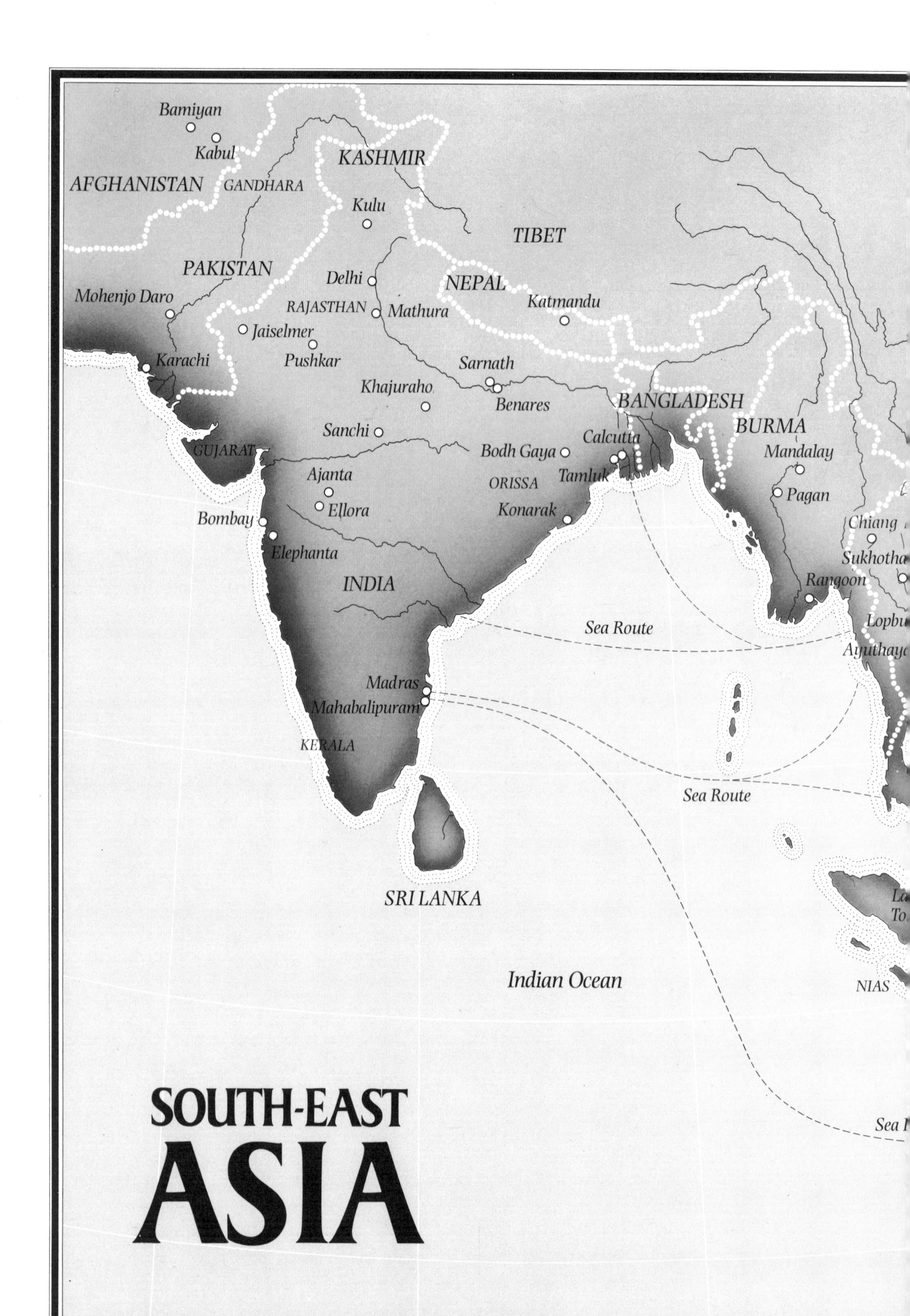

SOUTH-EAST ASIA